HOW TO WRITE AND PUBLISH YOUR FAMILY BOOK

by

Genealogy Publishing Service

448 Ruby Mine Road

Franklin, NC 28734

Telephone: (704) 524-7063

ISBN 1-881851-07-9

For additional copies of this book, contact:
*G*enealogy ***P***ublishing ***S***ervice
448 Ruby Mine Road
Franklin, NC 28734
(704) 524-7063

Made in the United States of America

Trademark Acknowledgments

TABLE OF CONTENTS

TABLE OF CONTENTS

CHAPTER I

GENEALOGY PUBLISHING SERVICE

GENERAL INFORMATION

GPS provides complete service for the preparation of typeset camera-ready book manuscripts and publishing of all types of genealogy and historical books. It is a family oriented business originally started by Colonel John T. Callicotte (USA-Ret), and now operated by Carl and Jane Moyer in Franklin, North Carolina. Many years of genealogical work and years of computer experience have now been added to the business.

The entire **GPS** effort is devoted only to the preparation and publishing of genealogical books including family books, autobiographies, historical, marriage records, censuses, cemeteries and other books of genealogy and historical matters.

One significant activity of **GPS** is the conversion of your family data into a camera-ready manuscript and printing of your family book. We can start work from your family group record forms, handwritten or typewritten material, computer printout, or computer disks. From this we prepare a typeset camera-ready manuscript. Using that manuscript, or one already prepared by you, we then print your family book with a hard or soft cover.

The objective of this guidebook is five fold:

1. To acquaint you with the services of GPS and explain how we can produce for you a quality genealogy book at an economical price.
2. To provide you complete guidance for preparation of your draft family book manuscript.
3. To provide you complete guidance for preparing your own, *ready for printing*, **camera-ready** manuscript.
4. To explain **GPS** methods of preparing camera-ready manuscripts for printing.
5. To provide basic information and general and cost guidelines for **printing** of genealogical books.

For the preparation of typeset camera-ready manuscripts, we are constantly upgrading our equipment and programs to take advantage of the latest technology. We are currently (1994) using one IBM™/PS2 Model 70-121 computer w/12mb of memory, 8512 VGA color monitor, 120mb hard disk, 3-1/2" high density disk drive, external 5-1/4" floppy disk drive and NEC CD ROM drive; one IBM™/PS2 Model 50 w/1.0 mb of memory, the 8512 VGA color monitor, 120 mb hard drive, two 3-1/2" high density disk drives and modem; one IBM™ 486/DX2-66 w/10 mb memory, SVGA monitor, 3-1/2 high density disk drive and CD ROM drive; and one Packard Bell™ 486SX-33 w/4 mb memory, SVGA monitor, 3-1/2 high density disk drive. The IBM™ Model 4029-10 Postscript Laser printer, the IBM™ Model 24XL Proprinter and a Hewlett-Packard Laser Jet™ handle the printing needs while the Hewlett-Packard™ Scanjet Plus scanner performs all the image and text scanning needs.

Following are a few of the current computer programs in use: Corel Ventura Publisher 5.0™, Word Perfect™ 6.1, DBase IV+™, Family Roots™, Family Tree Maker 2.0™, Roots III™, A&L Express™, Word Scan Plus 3.0™ plus utility programs such as Norton Utilities™ and XtGold™.

To take advantage of the latest technology in the printing area, the printing plant is continually updating the equipment in all of the plant departments including the photographic lab, press, trimming and folding areas, and the binding and packing areas. The net result is a high quality competitively priced book produced by a modern and efficient operation from beginning to end—*and all under one roof.* Many other book printing plants will subcontract the photographic and binding functions of book production.

In addition to preparing camera-ready manuscripts and printing of genealogical books, **GPS** can also assist authors of genealogy books in the preparation and distribution of pre-publication notices, collecting and accounting for pre-publication sales, distribution of the printed books and provide guidance on the financing of the publication of such books.

*Should the author so desire, **GPS** will obtain the Copyright Authorization and Library of Congress Catalog Card Number without cost to the author.*

It is the objective of **GPS** to prepare and publish genealogical books of excellent quality and beauty that will stand as a monument to the authors, their ancestors and their descendants. Authors are proud to autograph GPS products. Its foremost goal is to publish genealogical books of unsurpassed quality and beauty, and to increase its clientele of satisfied customers.

TERMS

Contracts are executed between **GPS** and clients for two of the three services provided, as follows:

1. **Preparation of camera-ready Manuscripts:**
   Terms for this service are as follows: One-third (1/3) upon execution of contract prior to start of work; one-third (1/3) when draft camera-ready manuscript is provided to the author; and balance upon completion of the final camera-ready manuscript including the alphabetical index and Table of Contents.

2. **Printing of books:**
   Due to our method of operation and low prices, terms for this are as follows: One-half (1/2) upon signing of the book printing contract and balance prior to shipment of books.

3. **Other services:**
   Packaging and mailing of books, printing of pre-publication notices, advertising, etc. will be billed after services are rendered.

Copies of our contracts forms are included in **Appendix G.**

Genealogy Publishing Service operates with low fixed overhead as a growing family business. The savings generated by this type of operation is passed on to its clients.

An Equal Opportunity Employer.

CHAPTER II

GETTING STARTED

GENERAL GUIDELINES

Sooner or later the family genealogist will want to convert all of the collected family data into a published book. This is a worthy and commendable objective for several reasons.

First—The author's ego and self-esteem will be enhanced by having his/her name as author on a beautifully bound family book of page after page of factual and interesting family data, by receipt of numerous letters of praise from known and unknown cousins, and by the inner feeling of knowing that when you passed through this world you left behind an everlasting memory for present and future descendants.

Second—unless the family data is converted into a published book, it is highly probable that the years of costly research, the volume of genealogical papers that were collected at much effort and great expense over a long period of time, will be relegated to the "*trash can*" by an uninterested heir.

Third—the exhaustive research has undoubtedly proven the existence of many living descendants of early ancestors who are interested in their "roots," and only by publishing the collected data will they be able to easily obtain such knowledge by simply reading a complete, organized and readable documentation—*your family book.*

The above presents three solid reasons for publishing of family data. Every person involved in the exhaustive effort of researching genealogy data will have their own reasons for wanting to see such data in publication.

ORGANIZING YOUR DATA

The **purpose of this guidebook** is to provide the knowledge and guidance believed necessary in obtaining a properly printed, top-quality book at an economical cost. To fully understand the contents of this guide, you should study and understand the **Glossary of Terms** in **Chapter V**, page 30, before reading further.

It is not the intent of this book to provide guidance on genealogy research, as local libraries have several fine books on that subject. There are also many organizations formed for that purpose. A local Genealogical Society exists in almost every County in every State in this Union. Some of these organizations are called Historical Societies. In addition to the County organizations, there are State Historical and Genealogical Societies. Take advantage of the expertise these organizations offer.

In all probability, much of your data was organized during the research period. The collection of such data and its transfer after collection to Family Group Record forms (available from Everton Publishers, Inc., P.O. Box 368, Logan, UT 84321, Order item #P6) will facilitate the organization of data along lines of descendency. The use of pedigree charts will also help in organizing data and will greatly enhance the final product.

5" x 8" ruled cards, obtainable at any office supply store, are also useful in recording and organizing your family data. Each card should be given a number and contain, like a Family Group Record form, all available information on a single family—with the husband's and wife's parents indicated by the number assigned to the parent's 5" x 8" card.

If the author is using, or plans to use, a computer to record and organize family data, it is suggested you obtain the **"FAMILY ROOTS"**™ program from Quinsept, Inc., P.O. Box 216, Lexington, MA 02173. 1-800-637-7668. This program is available for use on almost any type of computer, including IBM, Apple, MacIntosh, Tandy, etc. It will produce printouts in the Register, Modified Register and Henry formats. (See Appendix E for samples.) It can also be transferred to **"FAMILY TREE MAKER"**™ in order to print family charts.

In our opinion, **"FAMILY ROOTS"**™ outsells and exceeds in performance all other genealogy computer programs on the market. GPS has used the program extensively for over 5 years. It is a very versatile and flexible program, comes with a complete and easily understood User's Manual, is easy to operate via explicit screen menus, and has complementary features that substantially reduce key strokes when entering family data.

The program produces a variety of ancestral, pedigree and descendant charts, together with alphabetical and numerical listings of the computer family files. The program permits the inclusion of a text file of any length with each individual record. Using the basic individual's record together with the text file outlining the individual's personal characteristics, occupation, accomplishments, etc., the draft manuscript for your book can be written from the **"FAMILY ROOTS"**™ data on your computer. This will save you time and money.

Today, many families have a computer. If there is not one in your home, then perhaps some assistance can be obtained from a nearby computer-owner/relative to assist you in your project.

Once you learn how much easier your project can be accomplished with the use of a computer, we are sure you will become a proud owner of one. *Try it—you'll like it!*

In the event you don't desire to get acquainted with that newfangled machine and would rather stick to paper, pencil and/or typewriter, we again remind you of the use of Family Group Record forms or 5" x 8" cards. They can be a valuable tool in the organization of your data, by reducing the duplication of information, and assisting in the correct grouping of family data and related facts.

MANUSCRIPT OUTLINE

This is the most important step in writing the family history. Without an outline, the author is apt to wander from family to family, or from generation to generation—with the result that the final manuscript will be disorganized and difficult for the reader to follow or trace his/her ancestry. This guideline is based on the assumption that it is the author's desire to produce an attractive, well organized book that will bear a proud autograph.

Before starting the outline, the author must determine the scope of the book. How many surnames are to be covered in the book? Usually one. What has been the extent of the research? What are the principal objectives for writing the book? Who is the earliest ancestor? Does the author intend to only report his/her direct descendants or does the plan include the brothers and sisters of that early ancestor? What about the ancestry of their spouses?

Since the scope of a family book can be so varied, outlines cannot be suggested for every possibility. Perhaps the following will meet the scope of most family books. Presume that the research has been rather extensive. From this we arrive at the following scenario.

It was determined that the earliest traceable ancestor was John Ztupfx, who arrived from England to join the Jamestown Colony in 1607. John had four children, but little information is available on three of them. James, the fourth child, is a direct ancestor. James had four children: Charles, Henry, James Jr. and Mary Elizabeth. The author is a descendant of Charles, but during research, the ancestry of James' other three children was traced—thus accumulating significant amounts of data on each. The scope of the outline, therefore, is to include in the book, to the extent possible, all of the data collected on John, James, the four children of James, and their descendants.

In this case, however, the author wisely decided to include only spouses of the direct descendants of the Ztupfx surname, including their birth places and dates, and where available, the names of spouses' parents.

PREPARING MANUSCRIPT OUTLINE

Now that the scope of the book has been defined, the next step is to organize the data to best present an interesting and understandable lineage to the readers.

The most common data presentation format is to begin the book with the earliest known ancestors and work down to the present generations, chapter by chapter, including all known descendants. Don't presume for a second, however, that the names of all descendants will be obtained during the research effort.

Another common method is to divide the data by generations, having one chapter for each generation. While this presentation of data is good, it does result in duplication of data since parents must again be identified for the individuals in each generation. Chapters for this method are usually labelled "First Generation, Second Generation, etc." Your initial outline might look like this:

MY BOOK OUTLINE

CHAPTER I—Early ancestors including information on English Heritage, the Jamestown Colony, and John Ztupfx and his children, including James.

CHAPTER II—Charles Ztupfx and his descendants.

CHAPTER III—Henry Ztupfx and his descendants.

CHAPTER IV—James Ztupfx Jr. and his descendants.

CHAPTER V—Mary Elizabeth Ztupfx Harrison and her descendants.

APPENDICES

ALPHABETICAL INDEX

The first step in the book outline has been completed. Remember, the outline should be in sufficient detail that it practically and finally becomes a Table of Contents for the book.

The next step is to separate the voluminous research data into five drawers or boxes to correspond to the above chapters. Next comes the second step in preparation of your outline.

A review of the data in the box for Chapter II indicates that Charles had fourteen children. Volumes of data are available on eight of the fourteen. On each of the eight, there is sufficient data for thirty or more pages. The information available on the other six children is sufficiently small for inclusion in Chapter II, but to include the voluminous data on each of the other eight in that chapter would confuse the readers with too much family data in a single chapter.

Therefore, it is decided to add eight more chapters, one for each of the eight children. The initial outline is then revised as follows:

MY REVISED BOOK OUTLINE

TITLE PAGE

COPYRIGHT PAGE

TABLE OF CONTENTS

DEDICATION

PREFACE OR INTRODUCTION

CHAPTER I—No change

CHAPTER II—Charles Ztupfx and his Descendants.

CHAPTER III—Harriet Ztupfx, dau. of Charles Ztupfx, and her Descendants.

CHAPTER IV—Samuel J. Ztupfx, son of Charles Ztupfx, and his Descendants.

CHAPTER V—John R. Ztupfx, son of Charles Ztupfx, and his Descendants.

CHAPTER VI—Clyde M. Ztupfx, son of Charles Ztupfx, and his Descendants.

CHAPTER VII—Martha Jane Ztupfx, dau. of Charles Ztupfx, and her Descendants.

CHAPTER VIII—Henry S. Ztupfx, son of Charles Ztupfx, and his Descendants.

CHAPTER IX—Julia Marie Ztupfx, dau. of Charles Ztupfx, and her Descendants.

CHAPTER X—Thomas C. Ztupfx, son of Charles Ztupfx, and his Descendants.

CHAPTER XI—Henry Ztupfx and his Descendants.

CHAPTER XII—James Ztupfx Jr. and his Descendants.

CHAPTER XIII—Mary Elizabeth Ztupfx Harrison and her Descendants.

APPENDICES

ACKNOWLEDGEMENTS

ALPHABETICAL INDEX

Chapters XI, XII and XII may be expanded if the amount of data for these ancestors and their descendants so warrants. The point to remember when preparing this outline is to keep the chapters a reasonable length (75 pages or less). A chart (such as an organization chart) might be prepared and included at the beginning of each chapter for outlining the chapter and lineage as it appears in that chapter.

WILLS, ETC

Every author will undoubtedly have several wills that they would like to include in the book. GPS recommends that if there are many, that they be included as an Appendix in the book, with reference only to the specific Appendix within the text. Such wills, if handwritten, should be transcribed and presented in the book in printed format along with the copy of the will. Copies of Land Transactions, Tax Records, Lists of Marriage Records, and Cemeteries and their Internments should likewise be included as Appendices in the book and be transcribed into typewritten form, should the copies you have be handwritten.

The last thing to be included in the family book outline is the "Alphabetical Index." Much of the value of the family book is lost if the book fails to have such an index. More on this later.

At this point the author should accumulate all of the research data for each chapter into separate folders, i.e., all of the data on James Ztupfx Jr. should be placed in a file folder marked "Chapter XII," etc.

Remember, the book outline is a very flexible instrument, to be used, expanded and changed as the draft manuscript is written. It will probably undergo many changes before the manuscript is completely finished.

GENERATIONS CODES AND NUMBERING SYSTEMS

There are many systems for compiling your genealogy data to identify individual relationships and generations. You can use a descendant format as used by the National Genealogical Society Quarterly (known as the NGSQ System, the Modified Register System, or the Record System); or the Register System used by the New England Historic Genealogical Society.

The difference in the above systems is in the numbering of the children. The Register System gives a number only to children who have descendants. If, after compiling the descendants, you find that a child had descendants, you will probably have to renumber all the individuals. The NGSQ system numbers every individual whether they have any descendants or not. This system would not require renumbering if a child was found to have descendants at a later date. To show that an individual has descendants a "+" is placed in front of the individual's number.

You can use the outline explained on the previous page using the children for the chapter names. The numbering system can use that child as 1 and his children as 2, 3, 4, etc. Also, if you have substantial data on related families, you can create a chapter for each surname and start the earliest individual with number 1. Example of NGSQ system:

FIRST GENERATION

1. George W. **XTZRPMAN**^{1}. (Charles^{A}, George^{B}, Henry^{C}).

He married Alice **SWEASY**. Children:

+2 i. Earl Max "Bud"

3 ii. George

The numbers 1, 2 and 3 are identifying numbers for the individuals. The superscript 1 after George W. is the generation number. The letters A, B, C after Charles, George, and Henry show the pre-American generation letter. The + is shown to let the reader know there are descendants and further information. If there are no descendants, but there is further information on the child, it should be shown here as there will be no further reference to this child. The small Roman numerals i and ii show the birth order of the children. If an individual should marry a cousin, the cousin's identifying number would appear immediately after his/her name. This cousin would also appear with his/her family on another page.

Referring to the example above, the Register System would not assign a number to child "George," as he had no descendants. It would, however, keep the small Roman numeral ii. **A more detailed example of these two systems can be found in Appendix E, pages 51 & 52.**

There are also systems for compiling genealogies using ascending formats. The Sosa-Stradonitz or Ahnentafel system starts with the most recent individual and works back. The first person can be male or female. After that, the males are always even numbers and the females odd numbers.

Many genealogy computer programs can create the above numbering systems.

An outline system using paragraph numbering and indentation is shown on pages 47 & 48. This system can be used, but be aware that when a numbering system expands beyond five alpha and/or numerical characters it is confusing and requires a mind boggling interpretation by the reader.

If you use codes, the first character of the code, alpha or numeric, would indicate the generation. The second character of the code, alpha or numeric, would indicate the children, by birth sequence, for each individual of that generation. For example, return to the previous scenario and setup the following codes:

A-1: John Ztupfx

B-1-n*:All children of John Ztupfx

C-1-n*:All grandchildren of John Ztupfx

D-1-n*:All g-grandchildren of John Ztupfx

E-1-n*:All g-g-grandchildren of John Ztupfx

F-1-n*:All g-g-g-grandchildren of John Ztupfx

*The "n" represents the number of the child in the particular family. For example, the fourth child of John Ztupfx would be B-4.

This code can be easily expanded by one number or letter to further identify the separate children within each family. They can be identified with an additional code as follows:

B-4: James Ztupfx

C-4-1: Charles Ztupfx

C-4-2: Henry Ztupfx

C-4-3: James Ztupfx Jr.

C-4-4: Mary Elizabeth Ztupfx

The above examples and the ones in **Appendix E** are suggestions for formatting your genealogical data. Many authors devise their own systems or modify existing systems. The authors are the final decision makers as to what system they would like to see used in their books. Whatever system is used, be sure to give an explanation of its use in the front of your book.

TIME LIMITS

In addition to preparing the outline, which forms the road map for the actual writing of the manuscript, the author needs to establish time limits for the receipt of additional family data from many correspondents. Unless one sets a deadline and **sticks to it,** family data will be received for the book ad infinitum. GPS recommends the use of what is known as a "**pre-pre-publication notice**." Such should not be distributed until the author has completed his/her part of the research on the family and desires further identification on living descendants and their addresses.

This notice, which is sent to all known addressees, is advance notification that:

- The publishing of the book is in process.
- This is the last chance to participate in their own family history by providing family data.
- A deadline date is set for receiving such data and information received after that date cannot be placed in the book.
- A Family Group Record form is provided with advice to make photocopies for providing their information.
- They may send family photos that they would like in the book, although you, the author, will decide to use or not use such photos.
- Your name and address list is limited, so ask for names and addresses of all persons who might be interested in this Family Book.
- As soon as book publishing costs are known, a pre-publication notice will be sent to them providing an opportunity to order copies of the book.

Such pre-pre-publication notices generate increased interest in the family book, resulting in additional sales. In addition, a notice expands the author's address list for distribution of the pre-publication notice at a later date.

The important item at this point is to stick to that deadline even if the identity of, or information on, an important relative is still missing. Remember, a family book that is considered slightly incomplete is far better than no family book.

Genealogy Publishing Service prepares and distributes pre-pre-publication notices for its clients. Contact GPS for help on this subject.

GENERATING INTEREST

Many family books on today's bookshelves are dull, uninteresting, boring. Their contents, page after page, is largely limited to names, birth dates, death dates, marriage dates and places of these events. While such books may be accurate and complete genealogical presentations, they put the reader to sleep.

GPS wants every family book to be a genealogical gem. It should also keep the reader's interest, and provide him/her some insight to the character and activity of their ancestors. *How do you, the author, do this?*

First, don't be miserly with photographs. Pictures in a book create more interest than any number of words. The older the photos, the more interest. Everyone wants to know the appearance of their ancestors. But don't overlook photos of current generations. It is today's living descendants that will be buying the book, and their egos and interest will demand the presence on their bookshelves of any book that contains their photos. Of course, every individual in a family photo will want a copy of the book.

Suppose it does cost $9.95 for a half-tone to place one photo in a book. If 300 books are being printed, the cost per book for that photo is only $0.033 (3 ⅓ cents).

Another photo fact: It is well documented that a family book increases in value with age. Many unborn descendants for generations to come will have access to the published family books of today. Then your book will be an heirloom, a treasured possession that has been handed down from generation to generation. What unmeasurable pleasure the existence of photographs of their ancestors will provide these future generations.

BOAST ABOUT ANCESTORS

Photos are not the only item that can generate reading and purchasing interest in a family book. Include family anecdotes, whether they are legends, gossip or just rumors. Identify such as to their true identity—don't present them as facts unless they are known to be such. Boast about ancestors. Make their descendants proud of their heritage. Recite significant and well-known historical events that occurred nearby or during the life of an ancestor.

Define an individual's personal characteristics, whether or not current and future generations would consider such charateristics good or bad. *"John was a good and prosperous farmer, but he had a quick temper, was fond of alcohol and was a womanizer. These traits often caused him to spend the weekend in the local county jail in Suterville."* Or, *"George was convicted for killing the brother of a Judge, and was sentenced to five years in the Mississippi State Penitentiary in 1845. He died before completion of his sentence."* Or, *"Susan obtained her Master's Degree from Boston University in 1935, and her Ph.D. from Dartmouth in 1937. She was Professor of Mathematics at Syracuse University from 1940 until 1969, when she retired."* Or, *"According to his Civil War Military Record, Bill was 5'10" in height, had brown hair, blue eyes and was a farmer at time of his enlistment."*

A few of the items that can create reader interest are an individual's religion, occupation, places lived, property owned, political affiliations, military service, education, unusual or worthwhile accomplishments, and cause of death. Don't overlook including these items whenever the data is obtainable.

Some family book authors refrain from including marriage dates or birth dates when such would adversely reveal an out-of-wedlock conception. **GPS** feels that the inclusion or exclusion of such family data is a prerogative of the author. If **GPS** were the author, such data would be included, as it is believed that a family book should present all available facts. **GPS** has published books that included marriages of first cousins, marriage of brother to sister, unmarried mothers, suicides, murders, and other adverse family events.

In summary, as the manuscript is written, concentrate on making it interesting. Boast about those wonderful ancestors. Without them, we wouldn't be here. Thank God for ancestors.

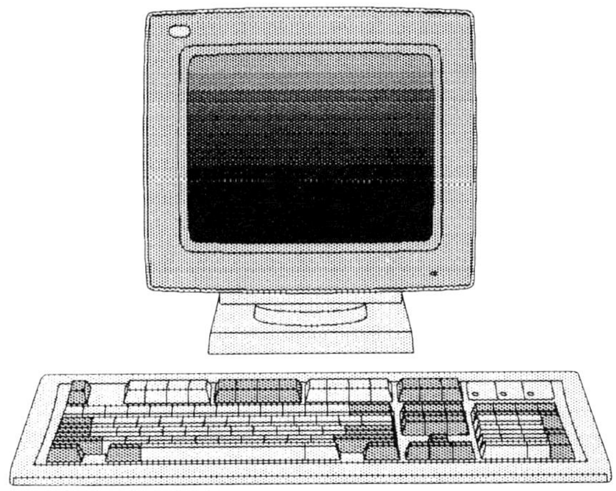
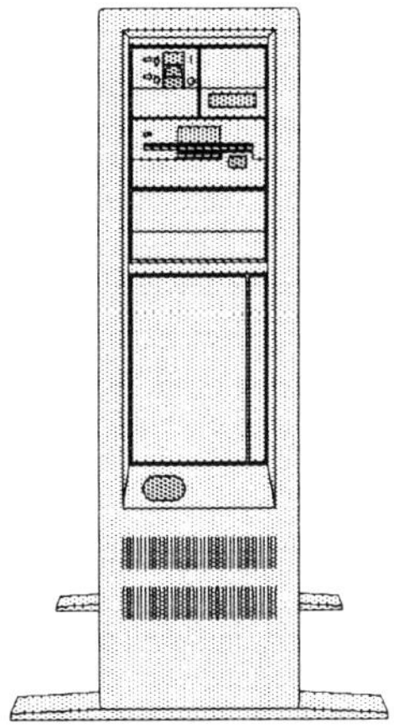
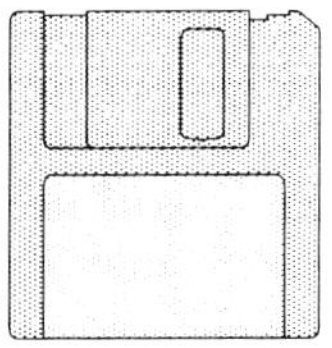

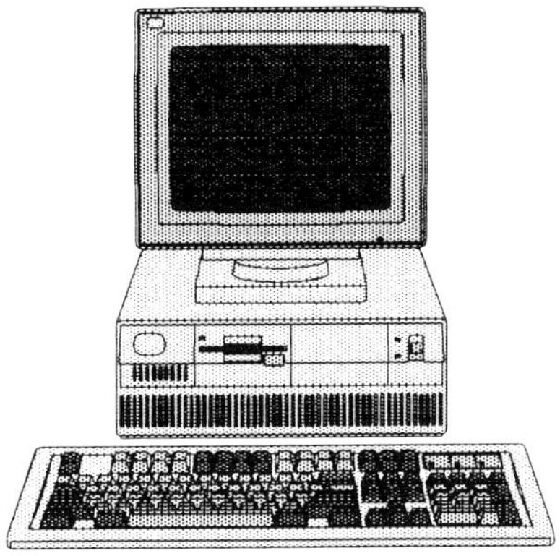
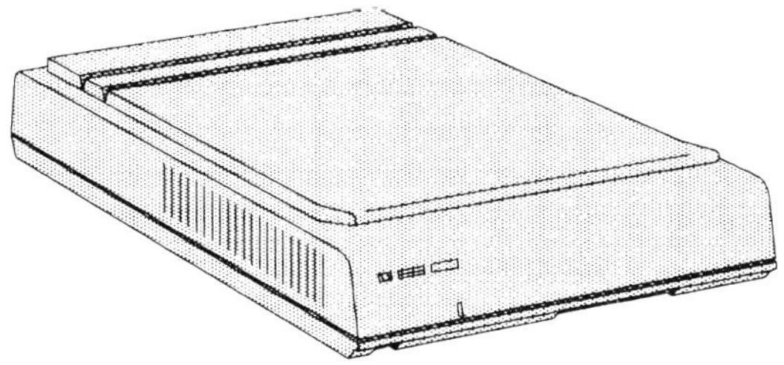
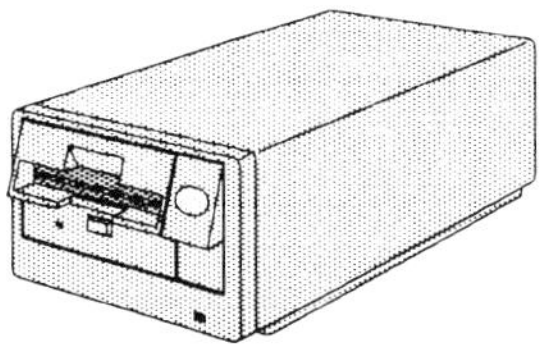

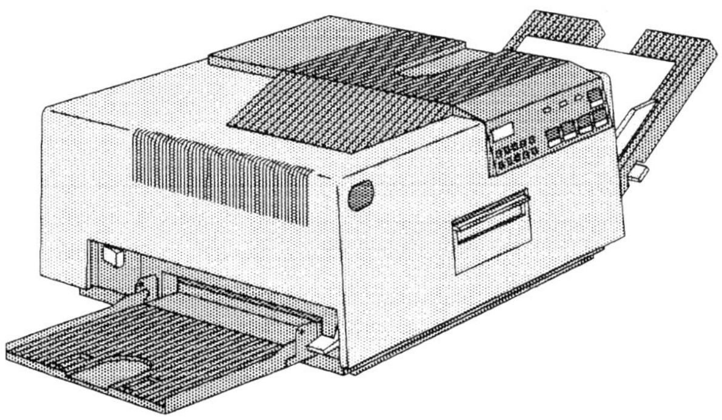

The above equipment is what will give you that "professional look" and will certainly make the job of producing a camera-ready manuscript easy to do! This is a small sample of some clip-art GPS has available in case you don't.

CHAPTER III

WRITING THE DRAFT MANUSCRIPT

EARLY THOUGHTS

Before the author starts writing the draft manuscript, a decision should be made as to the method and means for the preparation of the final camera-ready manuscript. Unless a decision is made at the beginning, duplicate and unnecessary work may result.

The final manuscript must be what is known in the printing business as a **"camera-ready"** manuscript. That is, it is complete in all aspects and ready for photographing onto printing press plates, with reduction as appropriate, for printing of the size of book desired. Authors should know at the start which of the following applies to their particular situation:

1. The camera-ready manuscript will be prepared on a typewriter.
2. The camera-ready manuscript will be prepared on a computer.
3. Draft manuscript will be prepared on a typewriter and camera-ready manuscript will be computer typeset by Genealogy Publishing Service.
4. Draft manuscript will be prepared on a computer and camera-ready manuscript will be computer typeset by Genealogy Publishing Service.

Authors should give serious consideration to having their camera-ready manuscript computer typeset by **Genealogy Publishing Service**. Such camera-ready output has that traditional typeset look without the high cost associated with the traditional expensive typesetting method. It is far superior to the output from a typewriter, dot matrix or daisy wheel computer printer.

GPS has over 1,000 typefaces that present a professional, high quality typeset appearance. This book is computer typeset using Times Roman 12 point font for most of the text. See sample typefaces and their sizes in **Appendix B.**

Once one of the typefaces choices has been selected, the author is ready to start writing the rough draft manuscript.

Start with Chapter I. Take out the folder in which you placed all of the research data for that chapter. Then refresh your memory on the information in that folder, organize your thoughts as to the order in which this data is to be presented, arrange the data in that order and start writing.

Whether handwriting or typing this draft, **double or triple space** to allow for additions and corrections. Leave wide margins at top, bottom, left and right as space for additions and corrections. Be sure that handwriting is legible, particularly as to the spelling of names, places and dates.

If the draft is being written on a computer, it is recommended that the printout be double spaced for editing of the hard copy.

Expect to edit and make changes several times to each chapter before deciding that the chapter is in final draft form—ready for preparation of the camera-ready manuscript.

It often helps to get a second opinion from a qualified relative or friend, if the author feels that the manuscript lacks clearness of expression, grammar or punctuation. The author may or may not want to accept their suggestions.

It is recommended that the author not try to finalize any draft chapter until all chapters of the manuscript are completed.

CHAPTER PARAGRAPHING

It is normally the practice that each **Chapter** of a family book is limited to the descendants of **one (1) ancestor**. Referring to our initial scenario, the heading for Chapter IV might be

CHAPTER IV
DESCENDANTS OF SAMUEL J. ZTUPFX

In the camera-ready manuscript, "CHAPTER IV" would appear at the top left margin of each left hand (even numbered) page, and "DESCENDANTS OF SAMUEL J. ZTUPFX" would appear at the top right margin of each right hand (odd numbered) page. When writing the draft, it is only necessary that the heading be placed on the first page of each chapter, regardless of which method is used for preparing the camera-ready manuscript.

When writing the draft, it is important that a consistent method of paragraphing and indentation be selected and maintained throughout the manuscript.

The author may desire to use the method explained in **Appendix D** of this book. That method provides not only clarity and easy readability, but it also presents an identifiable method of outlining descendancy within the chapter. A visual display of the paragraphing, sub-paragraphing and indentation, as explained in **Appendix D,** is shown in sample typeset pages in **Appendix E** of this book. An explanation of your paragraphing and indentation method should be included in the Preface of your book.

DON'T FORGET: If the draft is being prepared on a computer for future typesetting by **Genealogy Publishing Service,** and the author is using this proposed method or a modification thereof, do assign each paragraph its appropriate number, but do not use tabs to indent any of the paragraphs.

If any chapter includes information on more than nine generations, consider selecting one or more of the children *(as identified by paragraphs numbered I, II, III, etc.)* for additional chapters, by moving them to the heading of a newly formed chapter.

Our experience indicates that when any one chapter of a family book contains descendants for more than six generations, the chapter becomes confusing to the reader, with a resultant loss of interest and difficulty in understanding the lineage displayed therein.

There are instances, however, when voluminous information on nine generations is only available for one of the nine children (i.e., paragraph I or II). When this occurs, it is appropriate to include these nine generations in one chapter.

As explained earlier, writing a genealogy book is the **prerogative and responsibility of the author,** and includes the division of available data into chapters and into paragraphs within chapters, as desired by the author. The above is furnished for the author's guidance only, knowing that past experience has proven the above to be a highly satisfactory and acceptable method.

FOOTNOTES

In family books, footnotes are used primarily to show "sources of information." However, "sources" do not have to be limited to footnotes. For example, should the source of the information be a will, and a copy of that will has been placed in Appendix A of the book, a note in your text *"See Will in Appendix A"* would suffice without a footnote.

It is a common practice to list footnotes in a family book at the end of the chapter. This reduces the number of footnotes, since often the same "source" is applicable to more than one event or individual in that chapter.

The availability and identity of a footnote is indicated by a superscript number placed appropriately within the text. The following is an example within the text: *"Henry and Susan sold their 40 acre farm, located in Suskin County, North Carolina, on Little River in Aug 1860.*[1] *They moved to Hawkins County, Tennessee and purchased*[2] *a farm near his brother Charles. They had 4 children as follows:*[3]

At the end of the chapter, the footnotes might then appear as follows:

FOOTNOTES FOR THIS CHAPTER

1. Deed, dated 13 August 1860, Deed Book 5, Page 741, Suskin County Courthouse, Monroe, NC.
2. Deed, dated 12 January 1861, Deed Book 2, Page 16, Hawkins County Courthouse. Hawkins, Tenn.
3. U.S. Census, 1950, Suskin County, NC.

While writing the **draft** manuscript, place the superscript number within a circle at the appropriate place in your text, i.e., (1). On a separate page marked "Footnotes for Chapter ?" enter the number and footnote. Keep this page appended to the chapter pages. Those using a computer should consider keeping a separate disk file marked "Footnotes" with consecutive headings within the file denoting each chapter for which there are footnotes. This way all of the footnotes are in one computer file and can be easily found for each chapter.

PHOTOGRAPHS

The use of photographs in any family history serves to create an excellent book from an ordinary one. Photographs are half-toned individually, giving a quality as good or better than the original photograph. Without the half-toning process, the photo would appear as though it had been photocopied. However, there are certain considerations that have to be made when you decide to include photos.

Generally speaking, the finished book will be printed in black and white only, since color pictures are very expensive to print. If you are taking photos or requesting pictures from family members for inclusion in your book, the best results will come from black and white photographs. It is without a doubt best to let the book printer make the halftones from your photographs, since he knows his own equipment and how to get the best results from your photograph on his equipment.

PLACEMENT OF PHOTOGRAPHS

The task of placing and captioning of photos is certainly much easier when you are having the manuscript typeset by Genealogy Publishing Service. The only thing you have to remember is to number each photo and mark its number on your draft manuscript in the area where it is to appear. i.e. *"Photo #26 here."* Should the author have a particular desired size for the photo to appear in the book, add that information on the draft also, for example: *"Photo #26 here 2" x 2 ½"."* GPS will do the rest.

If you are preparing your own camera-ready manuscript, you must allow enough space for the size of the photo (allow at least 1/8" extra space around the top and sides) plus space directly below the photo for the caption. Use a different type style (bold and italics usually) for the caption and center it under the photo.

Remember, our plant photographer can reduce or enlarge your photo.

PHOTO NUMBERING

When you are certain that you are finished making changes to your FINAL CAMERA-READY MANUSCRIPT, place a 1" x 3" label on the back of the photo. Go through the pages and number the photos in the order you find them. Mark the photo label in a consecutive manner such as 1, 2, 3, etc. Avoid using 1, 1a, 2, 2a, etc. Mark the page number where the photo should appear on the same label. You should use a soft-tip pen when writing on these labels. Ball point pens and hard pencils sometimes will mark clear through the photo and appear on the final copy. It is also a good idea to make an inventory list and place a copy of it with the pictures.

Place the photo number and the size, in inches, that you want the photo to be, inside the boundaries of a box that you draw on the page they will appear on.

A rule of thumb is to place photos on left hand pages close to the left margin and vice-versa for right hand pages, unless the pictures are centered. Keep the caption centered under the photo, using ***bold and italics.***

MULTIPLE PHOTOS ON A PAGE

The cost of a half-tone is between eight and ten dollars (the cost is dependent on the finished trim size of your book) for one on a single page. The advantage to this way of doing it is that you will receive the highest possible quality of your picture. It is possible to place more than one photo on each page and then shoot the entire page as ONE PHOTO. However, there may be a slight reduction in quality overall. This can be kept to a minimum by selecting your photos that appear on the same page. In other words, you should use black and white photos together on one page and color pictures all on another page. Color pictures tend to be darker when half-toned. If you mix the two together, one or the other will be affected by the camera settings.

One other disadvantage is that you must put the photo captions on your manuscript page with the photos and then the whole page will be shot as one photo. If there is a reduction on this particular page, the caption will also be reduced, and vice-versa. Normally, this is not much of a problem if you place all of the photos and captions within the margins set up for the size of the book you are ordering. *(See Appendix C for appropriate margin dimensions.)*

MOUNTING OF PHOTOS AND CAPTIONS

We have seen several near disasters occur by using liquid adhesive or glue when placing photos or newspaper clippings on the manuscript page. The liquid goes through the material, marks the surface and shows up on the finished page. Scotch tape is another NO NO. A photo mounting board that has a sticky-front with a clear plastic sheet over it is also not good to use, as the plastic will cause distortions on the halftone. DO NOT USE THIS STUFF! The best thing to use that we have found is a glue stick (a solid glue sold in a tube, similar to lipstick, that you rub on the item you want to glue).

Be sure to place the pictures and the captions on the manuscript page as squarely as possible, and leave some space between them. Nothing looks worse than crooked pictures or slanted captions on a printed page.

If you desire color photographs printed in color, there will be an additional cost.

GPS will inspect each photograph for its quality for printing reproduction. If it is determined that the photo's quality will result in a poor book print, the author will be advised and given the opportunity to withdraw the photo from the manuscript. Generally, the printed photograph in the book will have the same or better quality than the original photograph.

Remember, the most interesting items in your family book will be the photos.

Sample of photo halftone and caption placement

MAPS AND DRAWINGS

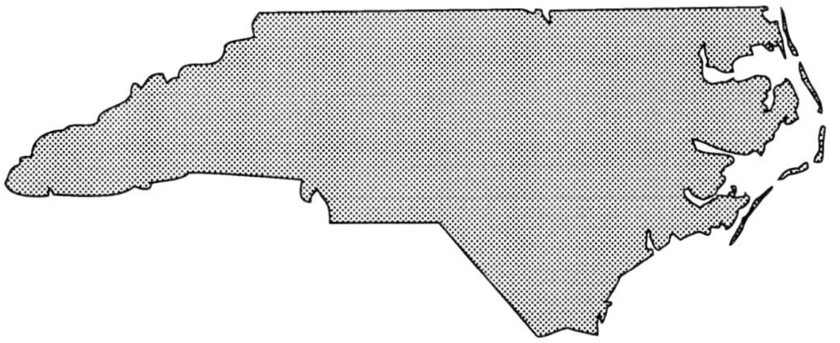

In addition to photographs, the author may want to include maps, land grants, drawings, etc., to add interest to the book. Maps of early ancestor homesteads are the most common. These may be early maps found in an archive, to which the location of the homestead has been marked. It is not uncommon to use a current road map in which the old homestead area has been pinpointed.

The author may want to include a handwritten will or deed to show readers how an original document appeared and to challenge their ability to transcribe such early American documents. The layout of a cemetery indicating where early ancestors are buried might also be included by the author.

Items of this nature may require a "line illustration" so that the document will be printed in its best clarity. Line illustrations are similar to, but not the same quality as, the halftones required for photographs. The cost of such is less than that for halftones.

PREFACE

The preface is a personal note or message from the author to the reader of the book. It is presented at the beginning of the book with the hope that it will be read prior to the reading of the book.

In the preface, the author can explain the reason for writing the book, give a generalization of the methods used for collecting the data, explain the hardships and thrills encountered during the research, explain the organization of the data in the book, explain abbreviations used, and define the generation coding system if one was used.

In addition, this is a good place to give credit where credit is due (this is not a book dedication) to those who helped with the project.

DRAFT PREPARATION REVIEW

Now for a basic review of the guidelines for preparation of the draft manuscript.

1. Prepare an outline for the manuscript.
2. Organize data and place it in drawers or folders according to the outline.
3. Review the data, prepare a revised outline, and reorganize the data into the folders for each chapter in the revised outline.
4. Place pertinent photographs, maps, drawings, etc., into the appropriate chapter folders.
5. Place wills, deeds, marriage records, etc., into folders for creating Appendices.
6. Write the draft manuscript, beginning with Chapter I. Review each chapter as it is completed, to insure that all available data has been included. Continue with each chapter, and then with the appendices.
7. Completely and thoroughly review the completed draft manuscript, looking for typographic, grammatical, and factual errors.

Once you are convinced that the above six steps have been completed—that the final draft manuscript is complete and correct, and that no additional data will be included (even if it arrives in the mail tomorrow)—then, and only then, you are ready to proceed to the phase outlined in the next chapter of this book.

This is what it takes!

CHAPTER IV

THE CAMERA-READY MANUSCRIPT

ANOTHER DECISION

Once the author has completed the final draft manuscript, the next step is to convert that draft into a camera-ready manuscript. Before working on the draft, the author made a decision that the camera-ready manuscript would be prepared by either (1) the author on a typewriter, (2) the author on a computer, or (3) **Genealogy Publishing Service**.

If the author selected **GPS**, his/her work on this project is completed. It is assumed that by this time the author has already forwarded to **GPS** some sample pages of the draft manuscript text and has obtained a cost estimate for typesetting the camera-ready manuscript and preparing the alphabetical index.

If so, then the author can package the draft typewritten manuscript, together with photos, footnotes, and appendices, and forward them to **Genealogy Publishing Service**. If the draft manuscript is on computer disks and the author has decided that **Genealogy Publishing Service** will typeset the camera-ready manuscript, then the floppy disks, along with a computer printout, should be forwarded to **GPS**.

In a short while, the author will receive, for final editing, a draft typeset camera-ready manuscript, formatted for all the photos and photo captions. When this **GPS** draft is returned by the author, **GPS** will make the corrections noted, prepare the final camera-ready manuscript, create the alphabetical index and the table of contents, and publish the manuscript as a hard-cover or soft-cover book, according to the author's specifications.

Should the author desire that the final camera-ready manuscript be published by another publisher, then **GPS** will forward this final manuscript directly to the author.

Before making the final decision as to the method of preparing the camera-ready manuscript, there are some facts the author should consider:

1. A typeset book has a professional look. This cannot be said of a book produced from a typewritten manuscript or from a computer printout using a dot matrix or daisy wheel printer.
2. The size of a book (number of pages) is reduced by an average of 20 percent when typeset.
3. A large part of the cost of typesetting is offset by a reduction in printing costs, due to the reduction of pages of a typeset manuscript.
4. If the number of pages and the number of books printed is large enough, the typesetting results in an overall lowering of the book's cost.

TYPESETTING COSTS

GPS has made it easy for the author to not only determine the cost of typesetting the camera-ready manuscript, but to see how the text would appear on a typeset page in the printed book.

1. If the draft manuscript is in handwritten or typewritten form, send GPS three or four pages of the draft manuscript text.

2. If the draft manuscript is on computer disks, send a disk with a copy of one of the chapter files along with the following information:

   a. Type of computer and program used to prepare the text file.

   b. A hard copy print-out of the text file. If the text file is in other than ASCII format and the author's word processing program has the capability to convert it to an ASCII file, please do so before sending it to **GPS**.

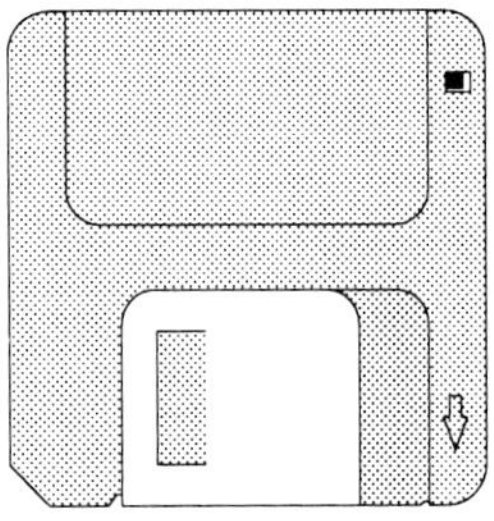

3. Advise **GPS** as to the trim size of the book to be published from the manuscript in order that the proper margins and size of font for the sample page can be determined.

From this information, **GPS** will, *without obligation to the author,* prepare two or three pages of typeset sample text. These will be forwarded to the author along with a cost per page figure for typesetting the entire manuscript—including preparation of the alphabetical index and table of contents.

Appendix E of this book displays some sample pages of family book texts that were typeset using the desktop publishing computer concept. The author may want to compare these to his/her typewritten or computer output, or use them as a guide in the preparation of his/her own camera-ready manuscript.

If the author has decided to prepare the camera-ready manuscript, the guidelines following in this chapter should be studied and considered. **GPS** uses many of these guidelines, and their use by the author will substantially improve the camera-ready manuscript and result in a more professional looking book.

PARAGRAPH INDENTATION

In **Chapter III** and in **Appendix D**, a method of paragraphing and indenting each paragraph and subparagraph is outlined in detail. It is presumed that the author will use this method or an adaptation of this method. It is suggested that the author reread the section on paragraphing in Chapter III.

Paragraph numbering is important during preparation of the draft manuscript. Indentation is not. Indentation, however, is important when preparing the final camera-ready manuscript. The appropriate tabs can be set on the typewriter or within the computer program to accomplish the desired indentation of each paragraph.

NUMBER OF COLUMNS

Normally, genealogical books use only one column to a page. This book was prepared showing both one and two column pages to give the reader an idea as to the appearance of each. **Appendix E** includes sample family book text in one and two column pages.

There are two factors to be considered when determining the number of columns to be used. They are:

- The personal choice of the author
- The amount of blank space remaining on most pages in the manuscript.

Blank space on a page occurs when lines of text contain only names or dates, for example:

A. John Ztupfx
B. James Ztupfx
C. Henry Ztupfx
D. Clyde Ztupfx

Blank Space

Notice all the blank space on the page to the right of the names—and this is a 2-column page. Even if a birth date were added after each name, considerable blank space would remain if the text were prepared on a 1-column 8 ½" x 11" page.

This blank space can increase the cost of a book, because it results in additional pages to contain the text. If the text includes numerous blank spaces of this type, then consider preparing the entire manuscript on pages containing at least two columns. Alphabetical indexes are normally prepared on pages that contain two or three columns, although we can use four columns on an 8 ½" x 11" page.

It should be noticed that this page has a vertical line between the two columns. This is not a normal practice in genealogy books, although it is another choice afforded the author. By the same token, horizontal lines below the heading and above the page number are frequently used. In this book, we've used a line below the page headings, but no line above the page numbers— *except on this page.* Again, such lines are a choice of the author.

MARGINS

When preparing a camera-ready manuscript, determining of the size of all four margins (top, bottom, left, right) is very important. Once set, these margins should be carried throughout the entire manuscript. To do otherwise lessens the book's appearance.

Margins must be established based on the planned size of the printed book. In addition to the size of the book, margins are also determined by the amount of photographic reduction the page will undergo to meet the book's trim size.

Normally, manuscripts for a planned 6" x 9" book that are prepared on 8 ½" x 11" paper will be prepared with margins that, when reduced 20%, will leave a ¾" margin at top, bottom and on the binding side and a ½" margin on the outside of the book page.

Manuscripts prepared for a planned 7" x 10" or 8 ½" x 11" book should be prepared, if possible, without a planned photographic reduction of the text.

Appendix C includes suggested margin layouts for most situations that will be faced by the authors of genealogical books.

TYPEFACES AND FONTS

Refer to the **Glossary of Terms** if you do not understand typefaces and fonts. Refer to **Appendix B** to view a variety of typefaces and fonts.

Typefaces are usually divided into two forms: serif and sans serif. This sentence is in Times, a serif typeface—it has fine cross strokes at the top and bottom of each letter. This sentence is in Helvetica, a sans serif typeface—it does not have fine cross strokes on the letters.

Typefaces may also be divided into fixed-space and proportional-space fonts. `This book is set in a variety of proportionally spaced fonts, except for this sentence, which is in the fixed-space font Courier.`

Typewriters are limited to fixed space fonts, such as Pica, Elite and Courier. With these fonts, each letter takes up the same amount of horizontal space—an "i" takes up as much space as a "w." Accordingly, these typefaces are known by the number of horizontal characters per inch. Elite is a 12 cpi (12 characters per horizontal inch) typeface. Pica is a 10 cpi typeface. If a typewriter has interchangeable typefaces, such as balls, thimbles or daisywheels, then typefaces other than Elite and Pica can be used. However, their sizes are still based on fixed-space characters per inch, usually 10 or 12, although a compressed typeface is available at 16 cpi.

Right justification of the text with a fixed-space typeface can only be accomplished by inserting additional spaces between the words in a line. This spreading apart of the words lessens the appearance of the text. Some computer word processing programs have limitations similar to the typewriter.

If at all possible, though, use proportional-spaced fonts—they are easier to read, and use less space than similarly sized fixed-space fonts.

Using a technique called "kerning," the horizontal space used by each letter in a proportional-spaced font can be increased or decreased. Kerning and proportional spacing are used together to obtain true justification of the right margin without the appearance of any added space between words or letters. This book and **Appendix E** present examples of this true right justification—a necessity for quality book appearance.

Those who use computers to prepare their camera-ready manuscripts will need to select fonts for their books—usually a serif font is used for the book text, and a sans serif font is used for headlines. Most serif fonts work with most sans serif fonts, but, in general, do not use two serif or two sans serif fonts. If you cannot decide which fonts will go together well, use just one serif font for the whole book and vary its appearance for headlines by using a larger size, bold, italic or all three. Don't, however, underline anything in your book when computer-typesetting. Use *italics* instead. **Genealogy Publishing Service** uses a wide variety of typefaces. Although New Century Schoolbook is most commonly used for body text, each book is given visual individuality by the use of different fonts for headings, chapter names, drop caps, title pages and book covers.

Typefaces come in various point sizes (72 points = 1" high). Each size is based on the height of the font and not its width. Select a font size of 10 to 12 points—11 points is best for 300 dots-per-inch inkjet and laser printers. The length of the typeset line also affects your choice of font size. For reading ease, the optimum number of characters per line is between 30 and 70, and so an 8 ½" x 11" page will require a larger point size than will a 6" x 9" page, unless the larger page has been set in two columns. Experiment with a sample page before you typeset your entire book, and then be consistent: use the same font, point size and leading for all your body text.

If the camera-ready manuscript will be photographically reduced to fit the final page size, a larger point size should be used. A 12 point font should be used when a 15% to 20% photographic reduction is required. If a reduction greater than 20% is required, consider using a 14 point font.

Some other computer typesetting hints: If you justify text, use hyphenation. Use only one space after a period, not two. DON'T USE ALL CAPS FOR LONG BLOCKS OF TEXT BECAUSE THEY'RE TOO HARD TO READ. Use open quotes (“) and close quotes (”) rather than inch marks ("). Use an m dash (—) instead of a double hyphen (--), with no spaces before or after it. Use an n dash (–) instead of a hyphen (-) for ranges, such as 1900–1975 and 3–5 years. Use an ellipsis (…) instead of three periods (...).

TEXT PAPER

Camera-ready manuscripts should be prepared on one side only of high quality, snow white, good opaqueness, 20# or heavier paper. **GPS** uses Hammermill Laser Print™ bond, a 24# snow white paper. There are others on the market of equal quality. Use only one side of each sheet. The final book will still be printed on double-sided pages during the printing process.

Regardless of the type of paper used, always start with a new, extra-black carbon ribbon (in a dot matrix or daisy wheel printer or in a typewriter), and replace it as often as necessary to retain the same print blackness on every page throughout the manuscript. An even better solution is to use an inkjet or laser printer—one rated at 300 dpi (dots per inch) resolution is sufficient. This results in a final book of the most professional appearance.

see
what
all the
noise
is
about

visit
your
Pinellas
public
libraries

AWARD-WINNING NIE PROGRAMS

THE TAMPA TRIBUNE
Newspaper In Education

your Pinellas public libraries

Clearwater Library System

Main Library
100 N. Osceola Ave.
Clearwater
(813) 462 - 6800

Dunedin Library
223 Douglas Ave.
Dunedin
(813) 738 - 4489

Gulf Beaches Library
200 Municipal Drive
Madeira Beach
(813) 391 - 2828

Gulfport Library
5501 28th Ave. South
Gulfport
(813) 893 - 1074

Largo Library
351 East Bay Drive
Largo
(813) 587 - 6715

Oldsmar Library
101 State St. West
Oldsmar
(813) 855 - 5940

Palm Harbor Library
2330 Nebraska Ave.
Palm Harbor
(813) 784 - 3332

Pinellas Park Library
7770 52nd St. North
Pinellas Park
(813) 541 - 0718

Seminole Library
9199 113th St. North
Seminole
(813) 397 - 2112

St. Pete Beach
365 73rd Ave.
St. Pete Beach
(813) 363 - 9238

Safety Harbor Library
101 2nd St. North
Safety Harbor
(813) 724 - 1525

Tarpon Springs
Craig Park,
Spring Blvd. S (before 1/97)
138 E Lemon St. (after 1/97)
Tarpon Springs
(813) 942 - 5613

Talking Book Library for the Blind and Physically Handicapped
12345 Starkey Road
Suite L, Largo
(813) 538 - 9567

St Petersburg Library System

Main Library
3745 Ninth Ave. North
St. Petersburg
(813) 893 - 7724

PINELLAS PUBLIC LIBRARY COOPERATIVE

FORMATTING FOR PHOTOGRAPHS

A square or rectangular blank area should be left on each page where a photograph is to be placed. With a typewriter, such blank areas can only be placed on the left or right margins of a page by adjusting the margins. The same is applicable to a computer using a word processing program.

Caption

When formatting for a photograph, be sure to leave sufficient space for the photo caption. Separate the caption from the other text, and center it under the blank area left for the photograph. If possible, use a different typeface for the photo caption, such as italics, script, or a typeface smaller than the one used for the book text.

PAGE NUMBERING

Should a computer be used for preparing the manuscript, the pages can be automatically consecutively numbered as they are printed. Most word processing computer programs present choices on placement of the page number on the page.

This selection permits placing the page number in the center bottom of the page, or on alternating bottom left and bottom right: on the right margin for odd numbered pages, and on the left margin for even numbered pages. *It is recommended that all page numbering be at the bottom margin of the page rather than at the top of the page.*

If the final camera-ready manuscript is being prepared on a typewriter, it is suggested that the page number be lightly marked on the back of each page as it is typed. Once the entire manuscript has been completed, reinsert each page and type in the page number, making sure that each number is inserted the same distance from the bottom of the page and is properly centered.

When using a typewriter, do not attempt to place the page number at the left or right hand margin.

Chapter I of the manuscript should start with page number 1. **All chapters should start on a right hand (odd numbered) page**. Book pages prior to page 1 (title page, Preface, Table of Contents, Dedication page, etc) should be numbered with alphabetical lower case letters representing the Roman numeral system: i, ii, iii, iv, v, vi, etc.

IMAGES

Images can further enhance the appearance of a book. Since it is normal that all chapters start on a right hand (odd numbered) page, this leaves part or all of the preceding, even numbered page blank. A portion of the preceding odd numbered page may also be blank.

Placing pertinent and appropriate images in these blank areas alleviates the stark whiteness. These blank areas can also be used for placement of one or more photographs, providing the photographs are of individuals mentioned in the text immediately before or after the blank area. Maps are appropriate on an even numbered blank page facing the beginning of a new chapter, and photos or drawings of a "home place" are appropriate anywhere.

GPS has a large assortment of clip art and wood cut images which can be used for this purpose without cost to the author. Representative images have been used in this book within the text to enliven the reading, and at the end of chapters to fill in the blank or partial blank pages. This is to give the reader an idea of the variety of copyright-free images available.

If an author wishes to select his own clip art, Dover Publications, Inc. (31 East 2nd Street, Mineola, NY 11501) has published an extensive assortment of copyright-free clip art and wood cut books which may be purchased at artist supply and book stores—or write to them for their catalog.

These images may be enlarged or reduced on a photocopy machine as necessary.

The use of images within a manuscript prepared by **GPS** is a prerogative of the author who must advise **GPS** whether or not images are to be inserted.

ALPHABETICAL INDEX

Using a Typewriter:

While the Alphabetical Index is part of the outline, it cannot be prepared until the camera-ready manuscript has been completed. To do otherwise could be a waste of considerable effort, as page numbers will change during the conversion of the draft to a camera-ready manuscript.

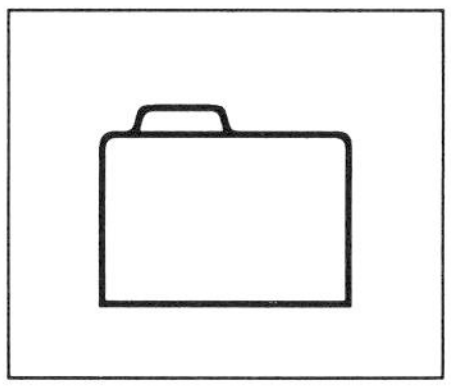

If the camera-ready manuscript is being prepared on a typewriter, consider using 3" x 5" cards for preparing the draft alphabetical index. Starting with page 1 of the manuscript, prepare one card for each last name on that page, and add all first and middle names with the page number to the corresponding last name card. Proceed with this exercise, page by page, keeping your cards alphabetized by last name.

Once cards have been completed on all surnames in the manuscript and all first/middle names with page numbers have been posted to each surname card, the alphabetical index can be typed. Depending upon the margins you use for your manuscript (See **Appendix C**), the alphabetical index can be prepared in either two or three columns per page. Placing four columns on a page using a typewriter is not recommended.

Using a Computer:

Today's more expensive and extensive word processing programs such as WordStar,™ Word Perfect™ and Word™ have the capability to self-generate an alphabetical index by marking each name during keyboard entry of the data. Many desktop publishing programs also have this feature. GPS has found that this method of index preparation requires so much attention during the typing, that numerous errors and omissions result. This type of indexing better supports the writing of technical manuals than of genealogical books, primarily because of the type of and greater number of index entries required for a genealogy book. Most word processors sort their indexes in RAM (memory), so if you have a large index, you may not have enough memory to create your index.

Another indexing option is to use, as GPS does, **SKY INDEX**™. This is a stand-alone program that creates indexes for family histories. With Sky Index, you simply read your manuscript and enter the topic (last name), sub-topic (first name), and page number for every occurrance of every individual in your book. Sky Index's data entry utilities are so easy to use, that you can enter all of your topics (last names) and sub-topics (first names) faster than you can code or tag them with your word processor. Sky Index displays the last record, added so that if all of the fields do not change you do not have to retype them. Sky Index also allows you to assign (and reassign) each function key to include either a first or a last name. This feature reduces typing time considerably.

Sky Index requires an IBM PC/XT, PC/AT or 100% compatible computer with a hard drive, 640K of RAM and DOS 3.0 or higher. Additional information about this program is available by writing to **Genealogy Publishing Service**. A demonstration disk is available by sending a check or money order for $5.00 to **GPS** and requesting a 3 ½" or 5 ¼" disk.

See **Appendix F** for sample indices.

Should the author encounter any problems in preparing his/her own camera-ready manuscript that are not answered in this chapter, please contact **Genealogy Publishing Service** for advice and guidance.

CHAPTER V

PRINTING YOUR BOOK

GENERAL INFORMATION

GPS books are printed using the offset lithography method. All books are printed to the author's specifications from a camera-ready manuscript at a competitive price. That manuscript may have been prepared by the author, by Genealogy Publishing Service, or by someone else employed by the author.

The author has the choice of selecting the type of cover (hard or soft), color and type of material for the cover, imprint on the cover and spine, type of paper for printing of the text of the book, size of the book, number of books to be printed (100 minimum), and shipping destination.

Books can be packed individually and mailed directly from the printing plant to names and addresses provided by the author. While most genealogical books are printed in black ink only, the capability exists to print in four colors. GPS books are printed in a printing plant using large modern presses. The complete printing process is performed under one roof, including all camera work, printing, folding, trimming, stamping of cover and spine, binding and shipping.

The goal of **Genealogy Publishing Service** is to publish genealogical books of excellent and lasting quality that will stand as a monument to the authors and their ancestors and descendants. This goal is continually met time after time as evidenced by the lack of even one dissatisfied customer.

At the request of the author, **GPS** also prepares, publishes and distributes pre-pre-publication, pre-publication, and after-publication notices or advertisments to be placed in magazines or newspapers.

COPYRIGHT

It is strongly recommended that all genealogical books be copyrighted. Should the author desire, **GPS** will obtain this copyright for each book it publishes at no charge to the author. However, two copies of the printed book will be required for forwarding to the Copyright Office. It is this act of publication with notice that actually secures copyright protection.

Having a book copyrighted does not prevent others from using the information therein, provided your permission to do so is requested and given. When giving such permission, it is appropriate to advise the requestor that *"permission is given, provided the source and author of the copyright information is shown."*

Almost all authors of genealogical books desire that a copy of the book be placed in the Library of Congress. To do this a Library of Congress Catalog Card Number is required. This number must be printed on the book's copyright page. **Genealogy Publishing Service** provides this service, free of charge, for the authors that desire their books on file in the Library of Congress.

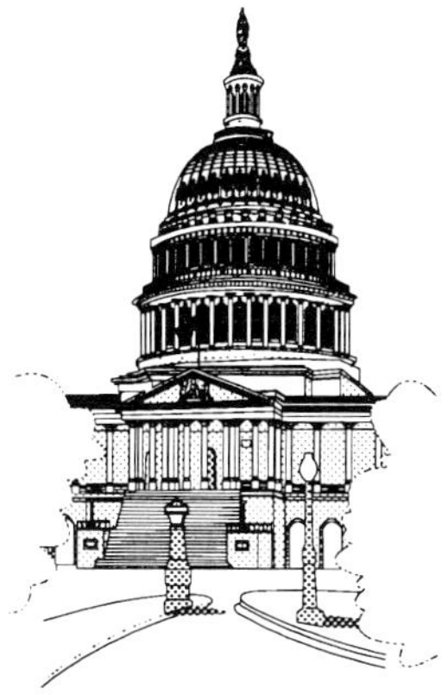

BOOK COVERS

Covers on genealogical books can be classified in two categories—hard and soft.

Hard Cover:

Because genealogical books are exposed to more wear and tear than other types of books, and because they have a much longer useful life, almost all are published with a hard cover. Unless 300 or more copies are being printed, a hard cover book costs less than a soft cover book. A hard cover book is a book that generally meets the following specifications:

The complete text of each book is bound with a top quality cloth or high quality cellulose fiber material in a choice of colors over a heavy .088" or .098" binder board (front and back). Covering the interior overlap of the cloth or fiber over the binder board is an 80# plain end sheet. Each signature is smythe sewn in groups of 32 pages, and first and last signatures of the book are reinforced. All signatures are then rounded and backed with headbands and footbands. The spine and cover are stamped with imitation gold foil using magnesium dies.

It is recommended that all hard cover family books be bound with Kivar 7 cloth or equal quality. Kivar is available in several weights, though the Kivar 7 is used most often. This is a beautiful leather look material, and comes in a variety of colors and textures.

Soft cover:

Everyone has been exposed to the soft cover, sometimes called "throw-away" or "dime novel" books. GPS soft cover books, however, are of much better quality than these dime novels. Not only is a higher grade of text paper used, but a heavier paper treated with a process called "Duro Sheen" is used for the cover. The Duro Sheen protects the imprinted impression on the cover from wearing off—even after extensive use. This soft cover is 10 point C1S—a very durable, heavy and long lasting paper cover. Soft cover books can be produced with or without the sew and wrap of the text pages. While slightly more expensive, it is recommended that the sew/wrap be used for all genealogical type books, again because of their excessive use and long useful life.

BOOK TRIM SIZES

Most genealogical books are printed with a trim size of 6" x 9". This size book fits most book shelves and is printed at less cost than larger size books. For example, a 288 page hard cover 6" x 9" book may cost $2636.00 for 300 books. The same number of books with 288 pages in 8½" x 11" size would cost $3988.00.

While the larger size book holds more text per page, thus reducing the number of pages for the same amount of text included in a 6" x 9" book, the resulting reduction of pages does not offset the increased cost for the larger book.

The reason for this difference is understandable. An 8½" x 11" book requires more cloth for the cover, larger binder boards, and more paper for the text. In addition, with a 6" x 9" page size, 32 pages will fit on one press plate. With the use of two plates, one for each side of the paper, 64 pages are printed with one pass of a sheet of paper through the press. Any size larger than 6" x 9" results in a 50% reduction of the number of pages per press plate. Consequently, the press run time, operator time, trimming time and folding time are all doubled for books larger than 6" x 9", resulting in higher book costs.

There is no intent to discourage the printing of larger books. GPS receives many requests to print 7" x 10" and 8½" x 11" books. Of these two sizes, the larger is more popular. Since all camera-ready manuscripts are prepared on 8½" x 11" paper, the printing of a book that size eliminates all the considerations necessary for reduction of the text and photographs and for determining appropriate margins. Of course with the guidance of this book, these problems are solved.

BOOK TEXT PAPER

Genealogical books are generally printed on text paper having a weight from 45# to 80#. This book is printed on 80# enamel, which is a high quality paper used for printing book text. The most common paper used for genealogy books is 60# Lakewood white. As the weight and quality of the paper increases, so does the cost of the book.

A significant trend in genealogy books is the move to acid free or alkaline paper. This paper is much more permanent (up to 200+ years) than acid paper. GPS uses only acid free paper in their books.

Book text paper is known by two factors: weight and pages per inch (ppi). Ppi is an important factor in selecting paper, as the width of a hard cover book is limited to 2½" and a perfect bind soft cover book is limited to 1⅞".

The following is a list of a few of the many types of papers used for printing genealogical books. These are listed in the order of cost from lowest to highest:

1. Lakewood 50#, White, Hi Bulk, 360 ppi
2. Booktext 50#, Natural, 490 ppi
3. Finch 50#, Opaque White, 606 ppi
4. Booktext 55#, Natural, Hi Bulk, 260 ppi
5. Lakewood 60#, White, Hi Bulk, 356 ppi
6. Booktext 60#, Natural, 408 ppi
7. Finch 60#, Opaque, 600 ppi
8. Finch 60#, Opaque, 474 ppi
9. Lakewood 70#, White, 390 ppi
10. Sterling 60#, Litho Matte, 550 ppi
11. Sterling 60#, Litho Gloss, 666 ppi
12. Sterling 70#, Litho Matte, 444 ppi
13. Sterling 70#, Litho Gloss, 572 ppi
14. Sterling 80#, Litho Matte, 400 ppi
15. Sterling 80#, Litho Gloss, 500 ppi
16. Dustjacket 80#, Enamel, 552 ppi

Any one of the above papers will result in a good quality book. There are many other types of paper used in printing books too numerous to mention here. The quality of the book increases with the increased cost of the paper used to produce it. There are lighter weight papers, but the waste factor offsets the lower cost, resulting in an equal or higher price.

Special Note: *When comparing book publishing prices obtained from different publishers, be sure you are comparing apples with apples. Verify that each publisher is quoting prices on the same type of cloth cover, the same type of book text paper, that each is providing bluelines, and that all other elements of the specifications for the book are the same or equal.*

DUST JACKETS

Dust jackets are like icing on the cake—beautiful, expensive and the first thing to disappear. They are usually printed in color on 80# paper (see previous page) and wrap around the front cover, spine and back cover of the book. Their reason for existence is to add appearance to the book and to protect the book's cover. Dust covers are only used on hard cover books.

Because of their price, and the excessive use and long life of a genealogical book, their use is not recommended for genealogical books. However, this again is a prerogative of the author, and GPS will print and wrap each book with a dust jacket when requested by the author.

BLUELINES

Bluelines, a printer terminology, refers to a printer's proof of the book. It is not supposed to look like the printed finished book. Its function is to provide the author a chance to review the pages prior to the actual printing of the book.

Bluelines afford the author the opportunity to check position of copy, correctness of margins, page alignment, placement of any illustrations and/or pictures. However, it is not meant to be proofread for typos, and it is not meant to give a true picture of the eventual quality of the printing or the reproduction of the halftones. Blues are meant to be scanned, not read line by line. Editorial changes in bluelines are unthinkable and expensive.

Blues, by the nature of the process, are apt to have specks and spots that show on the blue but are not on the negative (plate).

If you should desire to make a correction that is not the fault of **GPS** and results in a replacement page, there will be an additional per page charge to the author since, by prior approval, the author approved the final camera-ready manuscript for printing. Bluelines, after their review by the author, are returned to the publisher.

The cost of bluelines is approximately 50–60 cents per book page. This cost is included in all book publishing prices provided the author by **Genealogy Publishing Service**, as it is **GPS**' policy that the author have that last opportunity to review his/her book before it is printed.

NUMBER OF COPIES

One of the most important decisions to be made by the author is to determine the number of books to be printed. One of the best methods used to help make this decision is the "pre-publication notice." This is a notice sent to all known addresses available to the author that advertises the availability of the book and states as many details about the book as possible.

This notice should be prepared and distributed immediately upon completion of the camera-ready manuscript. At that time, the author will know the printing costs of the book, the number of pages, the number of photographs and all other details of the book, and can present all this information to potential purchasers. The notice should give the addressee thirty days to respond by completing an enclosed order blank and forwarding a check in the appropriate amount.

While the author must advise the publisher of the number of books to be printed when placing the printing order, this order may be adjusted at any time up until issuance of the bluelines. A significant decrease in the book order, though, may result in a price penalty to the author, as the printer may have ordered book materials, and any excess may not be usable in other printing jobs.

To avoid this very possible penalty, the author may want to wait to place the printing order with the publisher until returns are in from the pre-publication notice. This depends upon how anxious the author is to have the book published.

GPS' experience indicates that the author should order 50% to 75% more books than orders received as a result of the pre-publication notice. Why? Once the book has been distributed and seen by other relatives not previously ordering, additional orders will be forthcoming.

An author of a genealogical book should expect to receive orders for many years after the book is published. It could be embarrassing and disappointing if the author is unable to fulfill such orders. On the other hand, the author won't save anything by taking advantage of the low unit cost for 1,000 books if he has 800 of them stored in the attic ten years later.

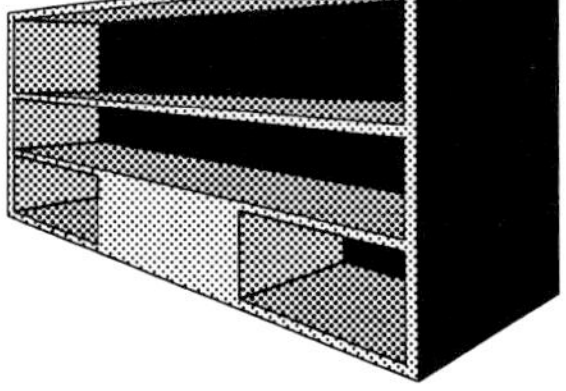

SETTING THE SALES PRICE

The publishing of a genealogical book is accomplished by the author for the sake of posterity, good will, a tribute to ancestors, and a gift to current and future generations. It is highly unlikely that the author will have a financial gain from such an undertaking. Certainly, the author should recover out-of-pocket expenses incident to preparation of the draft, camera-ready manuscript and the publishing and distribution of the book. Recovery of the costs incurred during research for the genealogy data should not be expected. The reason for this is the small quantity of genealogical books normally printed and sold.

Most genealogical books are printed in quantities of from 100 to 500. The setup costs for printing 100 books are the same as the setup costs for printing 10,000 books. The setup costs are a huge share of the total expense in the printing operation. If the author ordered and sold 300 or more books, the profit made should exceed out-of-pocket costs. As an example, if the unit cost for production of 100 books is $24.00, the unit cost for 300 books would approximate only $12.00. If the 300 books are all sold at the printing unit cost for 100 of $24.00 (a normal practice) then more than out-of-pocket expenses would be recovered. For this reason alone, authors should not hesitate to order books in excess of pre-publication orders.

In establishing the sales price by the author, four items must be taken into consideration:

1. cost to prepare the manuscript,
2. cost to print the book,
3. cost to package the book for mailing, and
4. cost of postage to mail the book.

The author will know the cost of the first two items after obtaining quotations from **Genealogy Publishing Service.**

The cost of packaging will largely depend upon the size of the book. Most books under 256 pages can be mailed in a #5 Jiffy-padded envelope or a #5 air bubble mailer. These cost from 75 cents to $1.00 each.

If books are larger than 256 pages, **GPS** can obtain regular book mailing boxes constructed to fit the exact size of the book. The cost of these will vary depending upon the size of the book and the quantity of books to be boxed. For estimating purposes, use $2.50 per book for this type of packaging.

The author can obtain a book corresponding in size to his planned book from his local library. Take that book to the Post Office, advise the postal clerk to add two ounces to its weight (for packaging) and compute the amount of postage required to mail that book using the Special 4th Class Book Rate.

Genealogy Publishing Service *can package and mail your books direct to those people who have ordered your book. This service is available for a nominal shipping and handling charge.*

PRINTING COSTS

For any publisher to provide a fixed printing cost to an author, the following information is required:

1. Specific number of pages in the book, including blank pages (a page is one side of a sheet).
2. Number of books to be printed.
3. Type of cover (hard or soft).
4. Type of text paper to be used.
5. Number of photographs.
6. Number of maps or other illustrations.
7. Shipping destination.
8. Other, such as dust jackets, tear-out or fold-out pages, other special items.

The price for printing books changes as a result of changes in costs of materials, overhead, and labor. Therefore, any book printing costs published in this book will be obsolete before the book is distributed. However, GPS feels that every author needs some yardstick book printing costs during the planning stage of the book.

Accordingly, the specifications and prices quoted below are provided only for the author's use during his/her preliminary planning phase. These prices should be used only as estimates and in no way bind GPS to a committed price schedule.

Hard Cover Book:

Unit cost per book, based on hard cover, Kivar 7 cloth (regular color and finish); 60# Lakewood White paper; smythe sewn rounded and backed; headbands and footbands; stamped spine and front cover with 1 impression gold foil. (Die for cover and spine not included in price. Shipping charges/freight also not included.)

Number of books

6" x 9" trim size

No. of Pages:	100	300	500	750
160	$15.89	$6.42	$4.52	$3.57
288	$21.66	$8.79	$6.21	$4.92
416	$27.52	$11.29	$7.92	$6.29
544	$33.28	$13.55	$9.60	$7.62
672	$39.11	$15.95	$11.30	$8.99
800	$44.87	$18.29	$12.97	$10.31

8 1/2" x 11"trim size

160	$22.59	$9.29	$6.63	$5.30
288	$32.47	$13.30	$9.46	$7.54
416	$42.27	$17.31	$12.32	$9.82
544	$52.20	$21.33	$15.17	$12.08
672	$62.09	$25.39	$18.05	$14.38
800	$71.88	$29.33	$20.82	$16.56

Soft Cover Book:

Unit cost per book, based on adhesive paper cover (soft cover), front cover and spine using black printing and 1 PMS color with Duro Sheen coating. Text paper is 60# Lakewood White, cover paper is 10 pt. C1S. (Prices do not include shipping charges.)

Number of Books

6" x 9" trim size

No. of Pages:	100	300	500	750
160	$14.44	$5.20	$3.36	$2.43
288	$20.09	$7.48	$4.97	$3.70
416	$28.50	$10.89	$7.36	$5.60
544	$34.13	$13.17	$8.98	$6.88
672	$39.80	$15.47	$10.61	$8.17
800	$45.47	$17.78	$12.25	$9.48

8 1/2" x 11" trim size

160	$16.88	$6.25	$4.13	$3.06
288	$31.19	$12.01	$8.18	$6.26
416	$40.71	$15.86	$10.89	$8.40
544	$50.25	$19.72	$13.62	$10.56
672	$59.81	$28.07	$16.32	$12.69
800	$69.38	$27.47	$19.09	$14.90

The above is provided only for your general information as to the cost of printing top quality hard and softcover books. When viewing these estimated prices, remember that these are top quality "library type" books. Please note the large reduction in unit costs as the quantity of books printed increases. As stated previously, the setup costs are a significant part of the cost of printing books.

PRODUCTION SCHEDULE

Orders are processed as received. Bluelines are normally furnished to the author from thirty to forty-five work days after receipt of the camera-ready manuscript.

Printed books are shipped, FOB the author's designated shipping address, 35 - 45 days after the receipt of the returned bluelines from the author.

There may be a few changes in this schedule caused by such events as annual plant vacations, unusual printing requirements from the author, discontinuance, or unavailability of requested type of cover cloth or text paper, and other unscheduled and unforeseen events.

SHIPPING

Books are bulk packed in single wall cartons for shipping to the author. Our shipping includes inside delivery to a residence. This means that the freight company delivering your books knows in advance that he is delivering the books to your home and must take the boxes off his truck and place them where you request. The inside delivery adds a little more cost to your quoted book prices, but saves you the hassle of dealing with a truck driver not willing to bring his truck down your residential street or to take the boxes off his truck.

OTHER TYPES OF BOOKS

If it is the author's intent to produce only a few copies (less than 100) and price takes precedence over book quality and appearance, then consideration should be given to multilithing or photocopying the completed manuscript.

Multilithing in lieu of lithography is a cheaper method of producing a family book. A local fast print shop is a good nearby source.

These books can then be bound in several ways. One method is binding with a wire stitcher, similar to a large stapler. Books are softbound with 67# cardstock and the cover is overprinted with the book title. The spines of the book are then taped with black bookbinding tape.

GBC is the brand name for **General Binding Corporation's** plastic comb binding. Books up to 2" thick and no longer than 14" can be GBC bound. The disadvantage is that the plastic is not as durable as other binding methods and the book cannot be doubled back past the point of lying flat. They are great when you have under 100 copies, but not worth the effort for anything over that amount.

Wire-O Binding is the brand name for a comb binding which uses a series of double wire loops from a preformed continuous wire. It costs about two to three times as much as perfect binding, because more hand labor is involved. The main advantage to Wire-O is that the pages lie flat when opened and the book may be doubled back on itself. Wire-O is best suited for computer/technical manuals and cookbooks. It is very durable and best used for books less than 7/8" thick.

Spiral is a type of mechanical binding which uses a continuous wire that is coiled or cork-screwed through round holes punched in the binding edge. It is used most often in notebooks and other manuals.

Saddle stitching means staples go through the crease of the spine, allowing pages to lie nearly flat when opened. This book is bound using saddle stitching.

There are many ways to bind a book. Which one you choose depends upon your design and budget as well as your requirements for durability.

GPS prefers using the hard cover because of its durability and good looks. This type of book will insure that your investment of time and money for researching your family history will be around for generations to come.

GLOSSARY OF TERMS

ASCII TEXT FILES: American Standard Code for Information Interchange. ASCII text is stored in exactly the same order as you see it on a printed page, with no additional characters added or deleted.

AUTHOR: One who makes or originates something, a creator, the writer of a book, article, etc.

BLEED: Printing that extends to the edge of the page after trimming.

BLUELINES: A proof copy of a book produced from a layout mask.

C1S: Paper coated on one side.

C2S: Paper coated on both sides.

CAMERA-READY: An author's copy of his written work fully prepared to be photographed for platemaking.

CASE BIND: See hard cover.

CLIP ART: High contrast drawings made to be cut out and pasted to a page can also be scanned to a computer disk.

COLOR SEPARATIONS: set of four half-tone negatives for making plates for 4-color process printing.

COMB BIND: To bind by inserting teeth of a flexible plastic comb through holes in a stack of paper.

COPYRIGHT: The exclusive right to the publication, production or sale of the rights to a literary, dramatic, artistic or musical work.

CROP: To eliminate portions of an illustration or photograph. This is done mechanically and does not damage the original photograph or illustration.

DIE: Block of metal used for embossing or foil stamping.

DUST COVER: A detachable paper cover usually gloss enamel used to cover a book.

END SHEETS: Sheets that attach the inside pages of a case bound book to its cover. Visible sides can be printed on, if desired.

FILM LAMINATE: Thin sheet of plastic adhered to printed paper for protection.

FOLD-OUT: A sheet folded one or more times (depending on size) that is attached to the book.

FONT: A unique combination of typeface, type size, type style, and type weight. For instance, Times Roman (typeface), 12 point (type size), bold (type weight) is one font; Times Roman 14 point is another.

FOOTNOTE: A note of comment, reference, or additional comment at the bottom of the page, end of chapter, or end of book.

FORMAT: The shape, size and general make-up or arrangement of a page, book or magazine.

4-COLOR PROCESS: Technique of printing that used the four process colors of ink.

GBC BINDING: General Binding Corporation's trade name for plastic comb binding. (Also see comb bind)

GPS: Genealogy Publishing Service, 448 Ruby Mine Road, Franklin, NC 28734.

GUTTER: Space between columns of type where pages meet at the binding.

HALF-TONE: A technique of representing shading with dots produced by photographing the object from behind a fine screen, or a photo-engraving so made.

HARD COVER: Any book bound in a relatively stiff cover, such as cloth-covered cardboard, as distinguished from paperback.

INDEX: An alphabetical listing of names or subjects together with the page numbers where they appear in the text.

ISBN: International Standard Book Number assigned to the book using a system administered by the R.R. Bowker Company. This number is used mainly when the book will be for sale to a large audience and will be available in book stores.

JUSTIFICATION: Text aligns evenly with both the left and right margins.

KERNING: Space reduction between specific letter pairs. Even when proportionally spaced, certain letter pairs should be placed more closely together to eliminate excessive white space. This space is especially noticeable with larger type sizes.

LEADING: The distance in points from the baseline of one line of type to the next.

LIBRARY OF CONGRESS: A National maintained library of extensive size for permanent retention of all books, articles etc., placed there by individuals.

LINE ILLUSTRATION: A drawing done entirely in lines from which a cut (line-cut) can be photoengraved for printing.

LITHOGRAPHY: The art or process of printing from a metal plate by a method based on the repulsion between grease and water. The design is placed on the surface with a greasy material, and then water and printing ink are successively applied; the greasy parts, which repel water, absorb the ink, but the wet parts do not. This technique produces high quality printing.

OFFSET PRINTING: A process in which the inked impression is first made on a rubber-covered roller, and is then transferred to paper.

OVERRUN: The number of books that were printed in excess of the quantity specified.

OVER SEWN OR SIDE STITCHING: Puts staples or thread through an entire stack of sheets near its edge. Pages bound by this method results in pages that will not lie flat when open.

PAGE COUNT: Total number of pages, including blank pages, introductory pages, and unnumbered pages.

PICA: A 12 point size of type the height of which is about 1/6 of an inch; a typographical unit of measure—6 picas = 1 inch; a size of type for typewriters that measures 10 characters to the horizontal inch.

PERFECT BIND: To bind sheets by gluing them, at the spine, to a paper cover.

PMS: Abbreviation for Pantone Matching System, a check standard for color reproduction and color reproduction materials, trademarked and owned by Pantone, Inc.

POINT: In printing, a unit of measurement for type, equal to about 1/72 of an inch. There are 12 points to a pica.

PREFACE: An introductory statement within a book that tells its subject, purpose, plan, etc.

PRE-PUBLICATION NOTICE: A notice sent to prospective purchasers prior to a book's publication to promote it and to obtain paid orders prior to committing funds for publishing.

PRINTER: A person whose work or business is printing; a device that prints; one who makes copies.

PROPORTIONAL SPACING: Different space is given to each character in a font. When proportionally spaced, the letter i requires less space than does the letter w.

PUBLISH: To produce, sell or otherwise make publically known; to issue the written work or works of a particular author; to announce, proclaim or divulge.

PUBLISHER: Webster defines a publisher as a person or firm that publishes; one whose business is the publishing of books, newspapers, periodicals; the coordinator between the author and printer to assist and guide the author in all aspects of the book and to properly guide and advise the printer to obtain the decisions made by the author.

SADDLE STITCH: To bind by stapling sheets together where they fold at the spine.

SCANNER: Device used to scan a page and load information into a computer for use in different applications.

SHRINKWRAP: Method of tightly wrapping books in plastic film.

SIDE STITCHING: See over sewn.

SMYTHE SEW: To use thread to fasten each signature together at the spine of the book.

SIGNATURE: A large sheet of paper on which are printed several pages in some multiple of four (4, 8, 12, 16, 32, etc.) and which, when folded to page size, forms one section of a book.

SOFT COVER: See perfect bind.

SPINE: Binding edge of a signature.

SPIRAL BIND: To bind using a spiral of wire or plastic looped through holes.

TABLE OF CONTENTS: A listing of the chapters or sections in a book.

TEXT: The actual structure of words in a writing; the actual or original words used by an author, as distinguished from notes.

TIP IN: To glue one edge of a sheet to another sheet or signature.

TRIM SIZE: The size, in inches, of the paper on which the text for a book is printed. The cover will be slightly larger to provide an overlap for protection of the text pages.

TYPESET: The act of producing a document on a typesetting machine or desktop publishing system.

TYPEFACE: The style of type, e.g. Helvetica, Times Roman, New Century Schoolbook, Courier.

Family Tree Maker for Windows 2.0

Organize your family information and print beautiful family trees with this easy to use software. Family Tree Maker automatically creates ancestor and descendant trees, birthday and anniversary calendars, mailing labels, cards, name tags and hundreds of reports. Now, version 2.0 stores any kind of family information including photos, scanned images, video clips and more. If you have a CD-ROM drive, you can even do research from the comfort of your own home with the CD-ROM Edition 2.0. This version includes an index of 100 million names of people who appear in state and federal records, such as the U.S. Censuses of the 1700s to the 1900s.

Genealogy Publishing Service has found this software to be exceptionally easy to use. The one outstanding feature is its ability to import from other leading genealogy programs, such as Family Roots, Roots III & IV, PAF and other programs that support the GEDCOM file format. **GPS** has used this program in several family histories, and we have found the charts and reports to be most helpful in displaying the lineage of a family in a simple and pleasing format. If the author really wants an outstanding book, this is one good way to accomplish just that! For more information about these programs, please contact **GPS** with your computer specifications at hand.

Following are a few sample charts and reports created with **Family Tree Maker 2.0:**

Descendants of George W. Xtzrpman

1 George W. XTZRPMAN Sex: Male
+Alice SWEASY Sex: Female Father: Mother:
    2 Earl Max XTZRPMAN Born: 1 Jul 1938 Sex: Male
    +Marjorie Darlene ZTUPFX Born: 24 Aug 1938 in Watseka, IL Married: 2 Mar 1957 Sex: Female Father: Mother:
        3 Roy Patrick XTZRPMAN Born: 15 Sep 1959 in Monterey, CA Sex: Male
        +Rosemary BIRCH Married: 4 Jul 1984 in Atlantic Beach, FL Sex: Female Father: Don Louis BIRCH Mother: Anne MILLER
            4 Roy Patrick XTZRPMAN, Jr. Born: 20 Feb 1987 in Jacksonville, FL Sex: Male
        3 Robert Dale XTZRPMAN Born: 15 Feb 1961 in Belleville, IL Sex: Male
        +Rhonda Sue WILLIAMS Married: 29 Nov 1985 in Jacksonville Beach, FL Sex: Female Father: Mother:
            4 Robert Daniel XTZRPMAN Born: 23 Nov 1985 in Orange Park, FL Sex: Male
        3 Richard Wayne XTZRPMAN Born: 27 Jun 1963 in Key West, FL Sex: Male
        3 Carl Ray XTZRPMAN Born: 31 Oct 1967 in Flat Rock, MI Died: 24 Apr 1971 Sex: Male

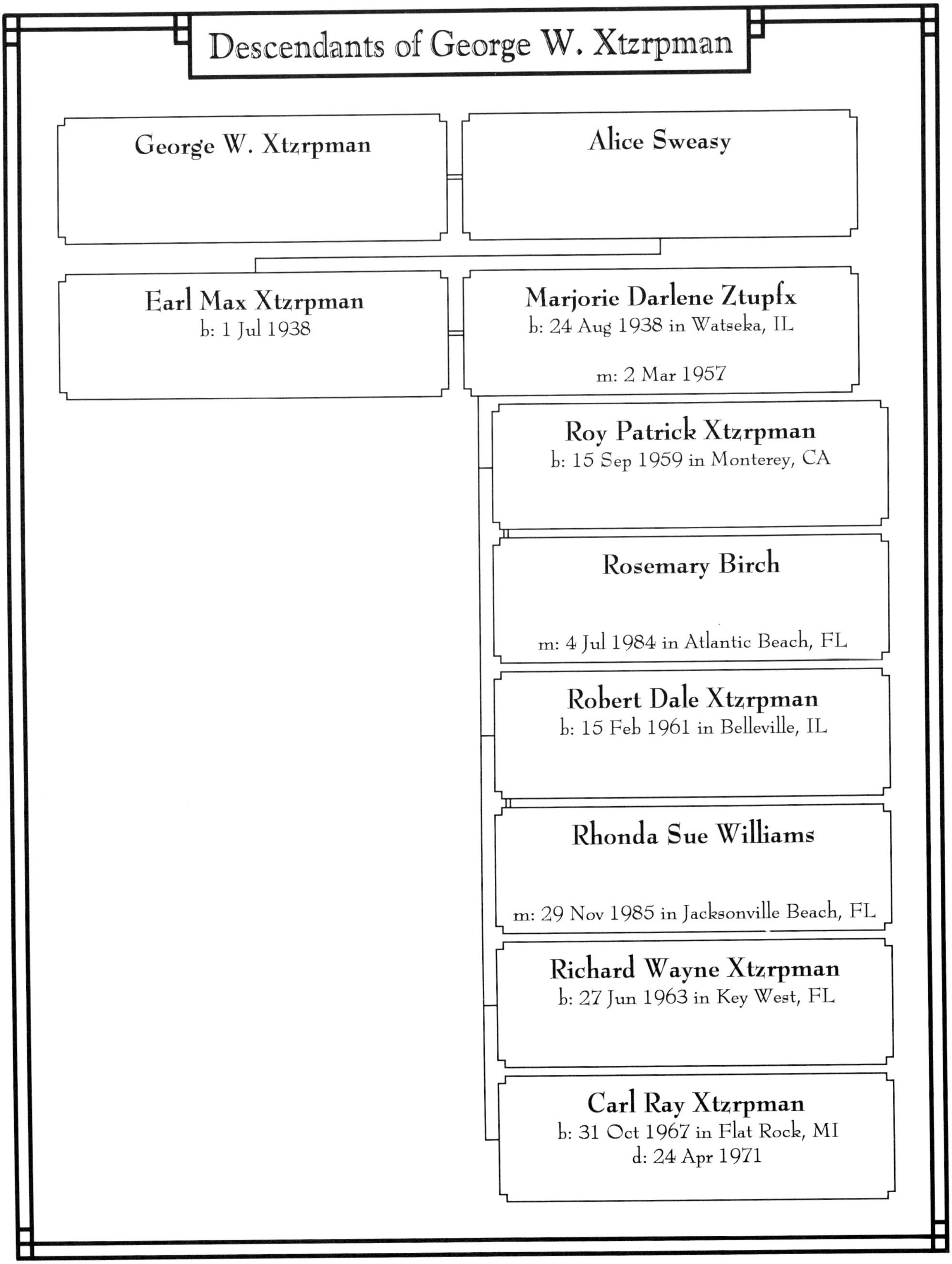
Descendants of George W. Xtzrpman
George W. Xtzrpman
Alice Sweasy
Earl Max Xtzrpman
b: 1 Jul 1938
Marjorie Darlene Ztupfx
b: 24 Aug 1938 in Watseka, IL
m: 2 Mar 1957
Roy Patrick Xtzrpman
b: 15 Sep 1959 in Monterey, CA
Rosemary Birch
m: 4 Jul 1984 in Atlantic Beach, FL
Robert Dale Xtzrpman
b: 15 Feb 1961 in Belleville, IL
Rhonda Sue Williams
m: 29 Nov 1985 in Jacksonville Beach, FL
Richard Wayne Xtzrpman
b: 27 Jun 1963 in Key West, FL
Carl Ray Xtzrpman
b: 31 Oct 1967 in Flat Rock, MI
d: 24 Apr 1971

Descendants of Frederico Sanchez Oramas

Ancestors of Robert Daniel Xtzrpman

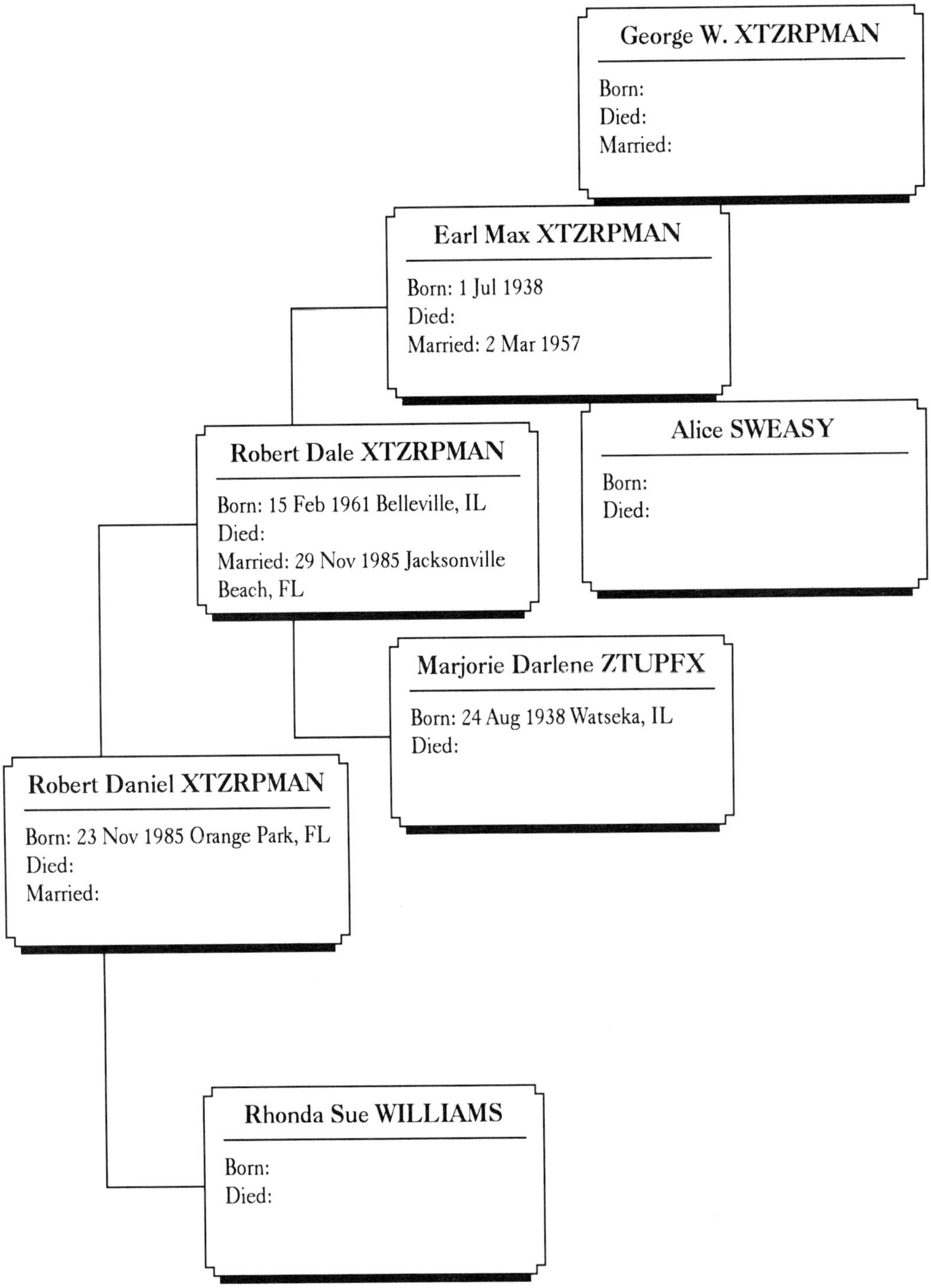

TIMES TYPEFACE
Font Sizes

Times is a proportionally spaced serif font. The following are some sample Times fonts available for typesetting camera-ready manuscripts.

TIMES 7 POINT: With this font we can also print in **bold** and *italics.* This font can be used for footnotes in manuscripts in which a 9 or 10 point font was used for the regular text.

TIMES 8 POINT: This size is also available in **bold** and *italics.* This size font can be used for footnotes when 9–11 point fonts are used for the text of the book.

TIMES 9 POINT: This font is also available in **bold** and *italics.* This size font can be used for regular book text when no reduction is required.

TIMES 10 POINT: This size font is available in **bold** and *italics.* This size font is excellent for book text when no reduction is needed.

TIMES 11 POINT: This size font is also available in **bold** and *italics.* Its size permits its use as an alternative to either the 10 or 12 point font.

TIMES 12 POINT: This font is also available in **bold** and *italics.* This is an excellent size font for book text when up to 20% reduction of such text is required to produce a smaller size book than 8½" x 11".

TIMES 14 POINT: Although shown here in bold, this font also available in normal **and** *italics.* **This size font is useful for headings and sub-headings.**

This is Times 18 point, **bold,** *italic,* ***bold italics,*** ALL CAPS.

This is Times 24 point, **bold,** *italic,* ***bold italics,*** ALL CAPS.

This is Times 30 point, **bold,** *italic,* ***bold italics,*** ALL CAPS.

These 18, 24 and 30 point fonts are useful for chapter headings, book covers, spines, and pre-publication notices. (This is 12 point bold.)

HELVETICA TYPEFACE
Font Sizes

Helvetica is a proportionally spaced sans serif font. The following are some Helvetica typefaces available for typesetting of camera-ready manuscripts.

HELVETICA 6 POINT: This font also available In **bold** and *Italics.* An excellent font size for footnotes when book text is no larger than 9 points.

HELVETICA 8 POINT: This font size also available in **bold** and *italics.* This size font can be used for text in an 8½" x 11" book that requires no reduction. Also useful for footnotes and references when used with book text of 10 or 11 points.

HELVETICA 9 POINT: Also available in **bold** and *italics.* This size can be used instead of 8 point to provide slightly larger text.

HELVETICA 10 POINT: Also available in **bold** and *italics.* This size is excellent for text that requires no reduction.

HELVETICA 11 POINT: Also available in **bold** and *italics.* A substitute for 10 point font when slightly larger letters are wanted, or for the 12 point font if slightly smaller letters are desired within the text.

HELVETICA 12 POINT: Also available in **bold** and *italics.* Ideal for book text that requires 20% reduction for production of a smaller book than 8½" x 11".

HELVETICA 14 POINT: Although shown here in bold, this font is available in normal **and** *italics.* **This size font is useful for headings and sub-headings.**

This is Helvetica 18 point, **bold,** *italics,* ***bold italics,*** ALL CAPS.

This is Helvetica 24 point, **bold,** *italics,* ***bold italics,*** ALL CAPS.

This is Helvetica 30 point, **bold,** *italics,* ***bold italics,*** ALL CAPS.

These 18, 24 and 30 point fonts are useful for chapter headings, book covers, spines and pre-publication notices. (This is 11 point bold.)

PALATINO TYPEFACE
Font Sizes

Palatino is a proportionally spaced serif font. The following are some Palatino typefaces available for typesetting of camera-ready manuscripts.

PALATINO 7 POINT: This font also available In **bold** and *Italics.* An excellent font size for footnotes when book text is 9–10 points.

PALATINO 8 POINT: This font also available in **bold** and *italics.* This size can be used for footnotes when a 9–11 point font is used for the book's text.

PALATINO 9 POINT: Also available in **bold** and *italics.* This size can be used for book text when no reduction is required.

PALATINO 10 POINT: Also available in **bold** and *italics.* This size is excellent for text that requires no reduction.

PALATINO 11 POINT: Also available in **bold** and *italics.* Its size permits its use as an alternative to either the 10 or 12 point fonts.

PALATINO 12 POINT: Also available in **bold** and *italics.* Ideal for book text that requires up to 20% reduction for production of a book smaller than 8½" x 11".

PALATINO 14 POINT: Although shown here in bold, this font is available in normal **and** *italics.* **This size font is useful for headings and sub-headings.**

This is Palatino 18 point, **bold,** *italics,* ***bold italics,*** ALL CAPS.

This is Palatino 24 point, **bold,** *italics,* ***bold italics,*** ALL CAPS.

This is Palatino 30 point, **bold,** *italics,* ***bold italics,*** ALL CAPS.

These 18, 24 and 30 point fonts are useful for chapter headings, book covers, spines and pre-publication notices. (This is 12 point bold.)

NEW CENTURY SCHOOLBOOK
Font Sizes

New Century Schoolbook is a proportionally spaced serif font. The following are some New Century Schoolbook typefaces available for typesetting of camera-ready manuscripts.

NEW CENTURY SCHOOLBOOK 6 POINT: This font also available in **bold** and *italics*. An excellent font size for footnotes when book text is no larger than 9 points.

NEW CENTURY SCHOOLBOOK 8 POINT: This size also available in **bold** and *italics*. This size font can be used for text in an 8½" x 11" book that requires no reduction. Also useful for footnotes and references when used with book text of 10 or 11 points,

NEW CENTURY SCHOOLBOOK 9 POINT: This font also available in **bold** and *italics*. This size can be used for book text when no reduction is required.

NEW CENTURY SCHOOLBOOK 10 POINT: This font also in **bold** and *italics*. This is an excellent font size for book text that requires no reduction.

NEW CENTURY SCHOOLBOOK 11 POINT: Also available in **bold** and *italics*. Its size permits its use as an alternative to either the 10 or 12 point fonts.

NEW CENTURY SCHOOLBOOK 12 POINT: Also available in **bold** and *italics*. Ideal for book text that requires up to 20% reduction for production of a book smaller that 8½" x 11".

NEW CENTURY SCHOOLBOOK 14 POINT: Shown here in bold, it is available in normal **and** *italics,* **and is useful for headings and sub-headings.**

New Century Schoolbook 18 point, **bold,** *italics,* ***bold italics,*** ALL CAPS.

New Century Schoolbook 24 point, **bold,** *italics,* ***bold italics,*** ALL CAPS.

New Century Schoolbook 30 point, **bold,** *italics,* ***bold italics,*** CAPS.

These 18, 24 and 30 point fonts are useful for chapter headings, book covers, spines, and pre-publication notices. (This is 12 point bold.)

5-3/4"

9-1/4"

This page reflects the margins that should be maintained for :

A camera-ready manuscript prepared on 8-1/2 x 11" paper which is to be reduced 20% for a 6 x 9" book.

Because of the 20% reduction a 12 point typeface will give best results when done on a computer, or Pica 10 cpi typeface should be used when manuscript is prepared on a typewriter.
(This box is printed with Times Roman 12 point bold.)

MARGINS

TOP: .... 1.00"

BOTTOM:......0.75"

LEFT: .... 1.50"

RIGHT:......... 1.25"

NOTE: Please include headings, footers and page numbers within these margins.

NOTE: The above left and right margins may be used both on right hand (odd numbered) pages, and left hand (even numbered pages, or:

Use the above on right hand pages only and reverse the left and right hand margins, i.e., set left margin at 1.25" and right margin at 1.50" for left hand pages. Either method is OK.

4-3/4"

This page reflects the margins that should be maintained for:

A camera-ready manuscript prepared on 8-1/2 x 11" paper which is to be published as a 6 x 9" book without reduction.

Since no reduction is required for a 6 x 9" book when using these margins, a 9 or 10 point typeface can be used if prepared by a computer, or, if prepared on a typewriter, an Elite 12 cpi or smaller typeface can be used.

7-1/2"

9"

MARGINS

TOP:	1.75"
BOTTOM:	1.75"
LEFT:	2.00"
RIGHT:	1.75"

The above left and right margins may be used both on right hand (odd numbered) pages, and left hand (even numbered) pages, or - Use the above on right hand pages only and reverse the left and right hand margins, i.e., set left margin at 1.75" and right margin at 2.00" for all even numbered pages.. Either method is OK.

Please keep headers, footers & page numbers within these margins.

6"

7" - Book Size

5-3/4" -Text Size

8-1/2"

10"

This page reflects the margins that should be maintained for:

A camera-ready manuscript prepared on 8-1/2" x 11" paper which is to be published as a 7 x 10" book. without reduction of text.

It is recommended that these margins be used for all camera-ready manuscripts prepared for a 7 x 10" book.

Since no reduction of text is required for a 7 x 10" book when using these margins, a 9 or 10 point typeface can be used if prepared by a computer, or when prepared on a typewriter, an Elite 12 cpi or smaller typeface can be used.

MARGINS

TOP:	1.25"
BOTTOM:	1.25"
LEFT:	1.50"
RIGHT:	1.25"

NOTE: The above left and right margins may be used both on right hand (odd numbered) pages, and left hand (even numbered pages, or - Use the above on right hand pages only and reverse the left and right hand margins, i.e., set left margin at 1.25" and right margin at 1.50" for all even numbered pages. Either method is OK.

Please keep headers and footers within these margins.

7.25"

9-1/2"

This page reflects the margins that should be maintained for:

A camera-ready manuscript prepared on 8-1/2 x 11" paper which is to be published as a 8-1/2" x 11" book without any reduction of text.

Since no reduction of text is required for an 8-1/2 x 11" book when using these margins, excellent results can be obtained if the text is computer typeset using a 9 or 10 point font. (This paragraph is printed in Times Roman 10 point normal. Also available in **bold** and *italics*.

If the camera-ready manuscript is prepared on a typewriteror or a computer not having a LaserJet printer, then an Elite 12 cpi or slightly smaller typeface may be used. This paragraph is printed in Times Roman 9 point bold.

Also available in normal and *italics.*

MARGINS

TOP:	0.75"
BOTTOM:	0.75"
LEFT:	0.75"
RIGHT:	0.50"

The above left and right margins may be used both on right hand (odd numbered) pages and left hand (even numbered) pages, or -
Use the above on right hand pages only and reverse the left and right hand margins, i.e., set left margin at 0.50" and right margin at 0.75" for all even numbered pages.
Either method is OK!

(Note that this is a left-hand even numbered page)

Please keep headers, footers and page numbers within these margins.

This page reflects the margins for a two-column page that should be maintained for:

A camera-ready manuscript prepared on 8-1/2" x 11" paper which is to be published as an 8-1/2 x 11" book without any reduction of text.

MARGINS

TOP:....................................0.75"

BOTTOM:............................0.75"

LEFT:...................................0.75"

RIGHT:................................0.50"

Each column is 3.5" wide with 0.25" between columns.

Since no reduction of text is required for an 8-1/2 x 11" book when using these margins, excellent results can be obtained if the text is computer typeset using a 9 or 10 point font.

(This is 9 point Times Roman bold and normal)

This is Times Roman 10 point bold. It can also be printed in normal 10 point Times Roman.
Italics can also be used. Leading (space between lines) can be adjusted for best readability.

If the camera-ready manuscript is prepared on a typewriter or on a computer not having a LaserJet printer, then an Elite 12 cpi. Lineprinter, or similar typeface can be used.

Please keep headers, footers and page numbers within these margins.

The reversal of the left and right margins as explained on the previous page is applicable for this 2-column page since the outside margins are the same.

This page reflects the margin for a three column page to be maintained for:

A camera-ready manuscript prepared on 8-1/2 x 11" paper which is to be published as an 8-1/2 x 11" book without any reduction of text

(Times Roman 10 pt)

MARGINS

TOP:........................0.75"
BOTTOM:..............0.75"
LEFT:......................0.75"
RIGHT:...................0.50"

Since no reduction of text is required for an 8-1/2" x 11" book when using these margins, excellent results can be obtained if the text is typeset using a 9 or 10 point font. This box is printed with a 10 point font.

Each column is 2.25" wide with 0.25" between columns.

Please keep headers, footers and page numbers within these margins

If the camera-ready manuscript is prepared on a typewriter or on a computer not having a LaserJet printer, than an Elite 12 cpi or even a compressed typeface font could be used.

PARAGRAPH NUMBERING AND INDENTATION

For the author's consideration, the following is a suggested method of paragraph numbering and indentation for use in a family book. This method is based on having a heading on each page of the chapter that indicates the ancestor's name, i.e., CHAPTER VI—CLYDE M. ZTUPFX. From this chapter heading, the reader knows that this chapter pertains to Clyde M. Ztupfx and his descendants.

While writing the draft manuscript, number, but do not indent, each paragraph. During preparation of the camera-ready manuscript, each paragraph is indented by **GPS** according to its assigned paragraph number. Samples of the use of this paragraphing and indentation method can be seen in Appendix E. This is the proposed method of numbering paragraphs and their indentation:

I., II., III., IV., V., etc.

    A., B., C., D., E., etc.

        1., 2., 3., 4., 5., 6., etc.

            a., b., c., d., e., f., etc.

                (1), (2), (3), (4), (5), etc.

                    (a), (b), (c), (d), (e), etc.

                        [1], [2], [3], [4], [5], etc.

                            [a], [b], [c], [d], [e], etc.

This is the numbering and indentation method used by **GPS** when not using a genealogy program with automatic numbering and indentation. Following is an explanation for each paragraph.

I. Using roman numerals I, II, III, IV, etc., at the far left margin designates that the name and information following in that paragraph pertains to the children of the individual whose name appears in the chapter heading at the top of the page.

A. Using upper case letters A, B, C, etc., indented ⅓" from the far left margin designates that the name and information following in that sub-paragraph pertains to the grandchildren of the individual whose name appears in the chapter heading at the top of the page and the child of the individual immediately preceding with a paragraph numbered with a roman numeral I, II, etc.

1. Using numeric numbers 1, 2, 3, etc., indented ⅔" from the left hand margin, is a sub- paragraph to the upper case alphabetical letters, A, B, C, D, etc., and designates the great- grandchildren of the individual in the chapter heading at top of the page as well as the child in the individual in A, B, C, paragraphs above.

a. Using lower case letters a, b, c, etc., indented 1" designates the children of the paragraphs numbered 1, 2, 3, etc., and the g-g-grandchildren of the individual in the chapter heading.

(1) Using numeric numbers in parentheses (1), (2), (3), etc., indented 1⅓" designates the children of the paragraphs numbered a, b, c, etc., and the g-g-g-grandchildren of the individual in the chapter heading.

(a) Using alpha lower case letters in parentheses (a), (b), (c), etc., indented 1⅔" designates the children of the individuals in paragraphs numbered (1), (2), (3), etc., and the g-g-g-g-grandchildren of the individual in the chapter heading.

[1] Using bracketed numeric numbers [1], [2], [3], etc., indented 2" designates the children of the individuals in paragraphs numbered (a), (b), (c), etc., and the g-g- g-g-g-grandchildren of the individual in the chapter heading.

[a] Using bracketed lower case letters [a], [b], [c], etc., indented 2⅓" designates the children of the individuals in paragraphs numbered [1], [2], [3], etc., and the g-g-g-g-g-g-grandchildren of the individual in the chapter heading.

At this point of the sub-paragraphing, information on nine (9) generations has been displayed in the chapter: I, A, 1, a, (1), (a), [1] and [a] plus the subject of the chapter heading.

Any matter of paragraphing and indentation is the personal choice of the author. There are many other methods, for example, your first paragraph could start with "A", or "1." Some authors prefer no sub-paragraph indentation. Some prefer not to number the paragraphs. In preparing typeset camera-ready manuscripts for the author, GPS follows the desires of the author as to paragraphing and indentation.

II. MARJORIE DARLENE ZTUPFX, b. Aug 24, 1938 at Watseka, IL. Darlene married Earl Max "Bud" XTZRPMAN on Mar 2, 1957. Bud, born Jul 1, 1938, is the oldest son of George W. XTZRPMAN and Alice SWEASY. Darlene and Bud had a "Navy life." He was in the Navy when they were married, and retired about 1976 with 20 years service. He was a radioman and teletype repairman performing sea duty in the Pacific, Atlantic and Mediterranean oceans, and shore duty at Monterey, Norfolk, Key West, Newport, and Jacksonville. In 1988, he works as a radio dispatcher for the Bar Harbor's Pilot Association in Jacksonville. Darlene and children accompanied Bud on each of his shore duty assignments. They had four children:

A. ROY PATRICK XTZRPMAN, b. Sep 15, 1959 in Monterey, CA. "Butch" graduated from Fletcher High School at Jacksonville Beach, FL, worked for some time for the State of Florida as a bridge toll collector, attended college, majoring in Computer Science, and on Jul 4, 1984 at Atlantic Beach, FL, married Rosemary BIRCH, daughter of Mr and Mrs Don Louis and Anne Miller BIRCH. They have a son:

1. ROY PATRICK XTZRPMAN JR, b. Feb 20, 1987 in the Baptist Hospital, Jacksonville, FL. He weighed in at 9 lbs. 4 oz., and measured 21".

B. ROBERT DALE XTZRPMAN, b. Feb 15, 1961 at Belleville, IL. After graduating from Fletcher High School at Jacksonville Beach, FL, he joined the U.S. Marines on Oct 21, 1980. After his hitch in the Marines, he was employed in an aircraft parts factory in Jacksonville, FL. On Nov 29, 1985 he married Rhonda Sue WILLIAMS at Jacksonville Beach, FL. They have 1 child:

1. ROBERT DANIEL XTZRPMAN, b. Nov 23,1985 at Orange Park, FL.

C. RICHARD WAYNE XTZRPMAN, b. Jun 27, 1963 at Key West, FL. Richard joined the U.S. Army in 1983.

D. CARL RAY XTZRPMAN, b. Oct 31, 1967 at Flat Rock, MI, died Apr 24, 1971 from a brain tumor.

III. MARSHA SUE ZTUPFX, b. Jun 15, 1945 in East St. Louis, IL. Marsha married Frank Edgar WILLIMS on Aug 1, 1964 at the United Church of Christ in Collinsville, IL. Frank, the son of Frank WILLIMS SR and Ruth CARRINGTON.

Sample text page which is to be reduced to 80% for a 6" x 9" book. Times Roman 12 point font was used for typesetting this page.

Lafayette, IN. Richard graduated from Ohio State University in 1987 with a Bachelor Degree in Accounting. On Dec 13, 1986 he married Lynda Susan Marklin, a senior at OSU and daughter of Mr and Mrs Charles Marklin. They were divorced in 1988.

B. HENRY THOMAS ZTUPFX, b. Dec 10, 1968 at Findlay, OH, a twin to John. This young man, a junior at Toledo University in 1988, is very interested and majoring in electronics.

C. JOHN JOSEPH ZTUPFX, b. Dec 10, 1968 at Findlay, OH, a twin to Henry. This young man, a senior at Illinois University in 1988, is studying electrical engineering.

D. LAURA DIANA ZTUPFX, b. Jan 13, 1970 on her grandfather's birthday, at Bryan, OH. In 1988 Laura is starting her first year of college.

II. GEORGE MERLE ZTUPFX, b. Mar 21, 1920 in Mt. Vernon, IN, the second child of Henry S. Ztupfx and Pauline Wilson. Merle completed elementary school at Caborn, IN, and subsequently enlisted in the Civilian Conservation Corps (CCC) with station in a camp near Edwardsville, IL. During this brief period of his youthful life, Merle and his older brother would visit each other's camps and put on boxing matches for the entertainment of the other enrollees. Neither of them were boxers but the audience was not conscious of that fact. He entered the U.S. Army on Jan 16, 1942 and during World War II participated in the Normandy, Northern France, Rhineland, and Central Europe campaigns as a member of General Bradley's Ninth U.S. Army. He was honorably discharged on Nov 19, 1945.

On Feb 24, 1947 he married Mary Catherine Sullivan, daughter of Michael Charles Sullivan and Gladys M. Burns of East St. Louis, IL. In 1972, Merle was employed by the Richmond Unified School District as a custodian. A few years later he was made head custodian of Tara Hills Elementary School in San Pablo, CA. He was a quiet, unassuming individual. He did not have the "Ztupfx temper," enjoyed his family, bowling, and professional baseball. Merle died of a heart attack at the age of 59 on Jan 21, 1980 and is buried in Rolling Hills Cemetery, El Sobrante, CA, next door to Pinole, where he resided at the time of his unexpected death. Merle and Mary had one daughter:

A. MARY CATHERINE ZTUPFX, b. Nov 26, 1960. Cathy married Gary Michael O'Rourke on Jul 7, 1979 in Berkeley, CA and in 1983 they own a home and live in Pittsburg, CA., and have a son:

1. GREGORY MICHAEL HILGER, b. Aug 16, 1985.

III. BESSIE MARIE ZTUPFX, b. Sep 29,1921 in Mt. Vernon, IN, the third child and oldest girl of Henry S. Ztupfx and Pauline Wilson.

Growing up as a member of a poor family during the great national depression of the 1930s placed a hardship and lifetime mark on children that even the poorest welfare families of the 1980s could not endure or imagine. This experience left a lasting impression on this generation—a philosophy of conservatism and sought after security. Upon completion of elementary school, and at the age of 14, Marie was employed as a sewing machine operator at the garment factory in Carmi, IL. One of that job's greatest disappointments was when they started deducting 1 cent from each dollar earned for social security.

This sample text page is prepared for printing, without reduction, as a 2-column 8½" x 11" book. Times Roman 10 point font was used for typesetting this page.

This sample page is prepared for a 6 x 9" book without reduction. This is 10 point font.

FIRST GENERATION

1. George W.[1] **XTZRPMAN**.

He married Alice **SWEASY**. Children:

+	2	i.	Earl Max "Bud"[2].

SECOND GENERATION

2. Earl Max "Bud"[2] **XTZRPMAN** (George W., 1). Born, 1 Jul 1938.

He married Marjorie Darlene **ZTUPFX**, 2 Mar 1957. Born, 24 Aug 1938, in Watseka, IL. Children:

+	3	i.	Roy Patrick[3].
+	4	ii.	Robert Dale.
	5	iii.	Richard Wayne. Born, 27 Jun 1963, in Key West, FL.
	6	iv.	Carl Ray. Born, 31 Oct 1967, in Flat Rock, MI. Died, 24 Apr 1971 (Died from a brain tumor).

THIRD GENERATION

3. Roy Patrick[3] **XTZRPMAN** (Earl Max "Bud", 2). Born, 15 Sep 1959, in Monterey, CA.

He married Rosemary **BIRCH**, daughter of Don Louis **BIRCH** and Anne **MILLER**, 4 Jul 1984. Children:

	7	i.	Roy Patrick Jr.[4]. Born, 20 Feb 1987, in Jacksonville, FL.

4. Robert Dale[3] **XTZRPMAN** (Earl Max "Bud", 2). Born, 15 Feb 1961, in Belleville, IL.

He married Rhonda Sue **WILLIAMS**. Children:

	8	i.	Robert Daniel[4]. Born, 23 Nov 1985, in Orange Park, FL.

This sample page is prepared for a 7 x 10" book without reduction. This is 10 point font.

FIRST GENERATION

1. George W.[1] **XTZRPMAN**.

He married Alice **SWEASY**. Children:

2 i. Earl Max "Bud"[2].

SECOND GENERATION

2. Earl Max "Bud"[2] **XTZRPMAN** (George W., 1). Born, 1 Jul 1938.

He married Marjorie Darlene **ZTUPFX**, 2 Mar 1957. Born, 24 Aug 1938, in Watseka, IL. Children:

3 i. Roy Patrick[3].
4 ii. Robert Dale.
iii. Richard Wayne. Born, 27 Jun 1963, in Key West, FL.
iv. Carl Ray. Born, 31 Oct 1967, in Flat Rock, MI. Died, 24 Apr 1971 (Died from a brain tumor).

THIRD GENERATION

3. Roy Patrick[3] **XTZRPMAN** (Earl Max "Bud", 2). Born, 15 Sep 1959, in Monterey, CA.

He married Rosemary **BIRCH**, daughter of Don Louis **BIRCH** and Anne **MILLER**, 4 Jul 1984. Children:

i. Roy Patrick Jr.[4]. Born, 20 Feb 1987, in Jacksonville, FL.

4. Robert Dale[3] **XTZRPMAN** (Earl Max "Bud", 2). Born, 15 Feb 1961, in Belleville, IL.

He married Rhonda Sue **WILLIAMS**. Children:

i. Robert Daniel[4]. Born, 23 Nov 1985, in Orange Park, FL.

SAMPLE ALPHABETICAL INDEX

(This style is used when typeset by GPS)

SAMPLE ALPHABETICAL INDEX

(Generated by "Sky Index" using 9 point Helvetica)

GENEALOGY PUBLISHING SERVICE
448 RUBY MINE ROAD
FRANKLIN, NC 28734

BOOK PUBLISHING CONTRACT

This agreement made this ______ day of ______________19____ between:

hereinafter referred to as the AUTHOR and Genealogy Publishing Service hereinafter referred to as PUBLISHER. The AUTHOR hereby grants and assigns to the PUBLISHER the right to publish the book at the AUTHOR'S expense.
Book title:____

The PUBLISHER agrees to print the book according to the following specifications:

The price for the above shall be____.
AS WITNESS, the hand and seal of the said AUTHOR and of the owner of GENEALOGY PUBLISHING SERVICE.
This ____________________ day of _______________, 19_____.

ATTEST:

______________________________	______________________________
(Author's Witness)	(Author)
______________________________	______________________________
(Publisher's Witness)	(Publisher)

Page 1 of 2

These two pages constitute the entire agreement between the AUTHOR and the PUBLISHER.

All camera-ready copy and other materials supplied to the PUBLISHER by the AUTHOR for inclusion in the AUTHOR'S book shall be clean, properly ordered and prepared in accordance with guidelines provided by the PUBLISHER. The PUBLISHER is not obligated to proofread copy.

Author agrees to pay the PUBLISHER at current rates for any additions, alterations or changes to the camera-ready copy other than what was originally quoted.

Bluelines will be provided to the AUTHOR along with a proof correction sheet. Corrections are to be indicated on this sheet which is to be signed and returned to the PUBLISHER. If any changes are necessary, AUTHOR agrees to pay for these changes or corrections.

Price quoted is subject to price increases for materials, including but not limited to paper, which may occur prior to final book shipment.

An over-run or under-run not to exceed 10% of quantities ordered shall be acceptable. AUTHOR agrees to pay for actual quantity delivered within this 10%. If AUTHOR does not wish any over-runs, an adjustment in the quoted prices may be necessary.

All copies of the book shall be printed under the imprint of GENEALOGY PUBLISHING SERVICE. The spine shall also bear the imprint of the PUBLISHER.

A Library of Congress Catalog Card Number will be obtained for the AUTHOR and this number placed on the flypage. The PUBLISHER will also send the required one (1) copy of the book to the Library of Congress. Book to be supplied by AUTHOR.

The PUBLISHER will register the book with the Register of Copyrights, taking the registration out in the name of the AUTHOR. The PUBLISHER will also send the required two (2) copies of the book along with the registration. The original registration form will be mailed to the AUTHOR upon its receipt from the Copyright Office. Books to be supplied by AUTHOR.

Unless otherwise noted, the price quoted is for a single prepaid delivery of books to the AUTHOR'S designated address. Unless specified, individual shipping of books including postage and handling is not included. Postage, freight and other handling charges for shipping individual books will be charged at current rates and billed separately.

Barring delays which are neither the fault of the AUTHOR nor the PUBLISHER, the books shall be ready for shipment within ________________ of the receipt of the camera-ready manuscript and the signing of this contract.

Payment shall be made as follows: one-half of the stated contract price with order, and balance due when the books are ready for shipment.

State sales tax will be charged according to the rate in effect in the state the books are shipped to, unless a copy of the AUTHOR'S tax certificate and/or number is on file with the PUBLISHER.

The AUTHOR warrants that the book to be published is original (unless a reprint is noted) and is no way an infringement of the copyrights of others, or the laws governing copyrights. The AUTHOR further warrants that he will not submit for publication any matter that is libelous or otherwise actionable, and that the PUBLISHER shall have the exclusive right, after advising the AUTHOR, to refuse to include such matter in the book. The PUBLISHER'S rights hereunder shall not relieve the AUTHOR from any and all liability both to the PUBLISHER and to the Public for publication of any matter contained in the book that is libelous or otherwise actionable as aforesaid; and the AUTHOR agrees to indemnify the PUBLISHER, its successors and assigns, for any losses, costs or damages which it may suffer by reason of the matters mentioned in this paragraph.

Whenever feasible, the AUTHOR shall retain copies of all manuscripts and illustrations and/or photographs delivered to the PUBLISHER. The PUBLISHER shall exercise all due care of the manuscript and illustrations and/or photographs, but the PUBLISHER shall incur no liability to the AUTHOR because of the loss of, theft of, or damage to the said material while in the PUBLISHER'S possession; nor because of the PUBLISHER'S inability to go forward with publication by reason of said loss, theft, or damage. However, where camera-ready copy has been supplied to or produced by the PUBLISHER, and such copy is lost, stolen, or damaged, then the PUBLISHER shall replace said copy at PUBLISHER'S expense and the AUTHOR agrees to furnish a duplicate manuscript for the purpose of such composition.

This contract shall be binding upon the parties hereto, their heirs, successors, assigns and personal representatives. This contract shall be construed and enforced in accordance with the laws of the State of North Carolina.

Page 2 of 2

GENEALOGY PUBLISHING SERVICE
448 RUBY MINE ROAD
FRANKLIN, NC 28734

MANUSCRIPT PREPARATION CONTRACT

This agreement, made this ________________ day of ____________________ 19____, between:

hereinafter referred to as the AUTHOR, hereby agrees to provide to GENEALOGY PUBLISHING SERVICE, hereinafter referred to as GPS, a draft manuscript. The manuscript consists of the following:

Number of Pages:_________ Number of Photographs:_________

GPS agrees to prepare such camera-ready manuscript under the following terms and conditions:

1. If the draft manuscript is provided in computer disk format, the AUTHOR will also provide GPS a computer printout of each computer file arranged in the order they are to appear in the finished camera-ready manuscript and advise GPS the make and model of computer and computer programs used in preparation of the computer disks.These files are to be proofed, for any errors, by the AUTHOR prior to delivery to GPS. GPS will not be expected to do proofing or editing as this is the AUTHOR'S responsibility.

2. A draft copy of the camera-ready manuscript will be provided the AUTHOR for the purpose of editing and return to GPS. Editing will be for the purpose of correcting, by the AUTHOR, any errors and omissions made by GPS and may include corrections or additions to correct errors or omissions made in the original draft manuscript by the AUTHOR. This draft camera-ready manuscript is to be returned to GPS within a reasonable number of days, not in excess of 30, from receipt by the AUTHOR.

3. All corrections indicated by the editing of the draft copy by the AUTHOR will be made, and a final camera-ready manuscript will be prepared by GPS. The final camera-ready manuscript will be prepared on high quality snow white 24#, 8½" x 11" paper to assure best printing quality.

4. Should the AUTHOR desire to edit the camera-ready manuscript and submits further corrections to be made by GPS, which were not the fault of GPS, then a charge will be made equal to the charge per page for preparation of the camera-ready manuscript.

5. Upon completion of the final camera-ready manuscript, an alphabetical index, table of contents, title page and copyright page will be included. The alphabetical index will show alphabetically the last name, first name and page number of every individual listed in the final manuscript.

6. The final camera-ready manuscript will be of a quality previously indicated and agreed to by the AUTHOR from samples or communications provided by GPS. GPS will make every effort to comply with he wishes of the AUTHOR as they pertain to page format, numbering, paragraphing and photograph presentation, but reserves the right and privilege of determining the page format, numbering, paragraphing and picture presentation if, in the opinion of GPS, the exercise of such right and privilege is necessary to present a professional appearance to the published book and to maintain the standard of GPS quality.

7. GPS will exercise all due care against loss, theft or damage to the AUTHOR'S draft manuscript and illustrations, but GPS shall incur no liability to the AUTHOR because of the loss, theft, or damage to said material while in the possession of GPS. Whenever, feasible, the AUTHOR should retain copies of all manuscript and illustrations delivered to GPS.

Page 1 of 2

8. Barring delays which are neither the fault of the AUTHOR nor GPS, the draft camera-ready manuscript will be provided the AUTHOR for edit within _____ days after receipt of the AUTHOR'S draft manuscript. The final camera-ready manuscript and alphabetical index will be available for publishing within _____ days after return of the draft camera-ready manuscript by the AUTHOR. This schedule is subject to change dependent upon receipt of any additional material for inclusion in manuscript.

The price for preparation of said camera-ready manuscript shall be as follows:

Estimated number of pages is ______________. Cost per final camera-ready manuscript page of $______________. Estimated total cost for pages $______________.

Cost of $1.50 for formatting the page and entering the photo caption for each photograph or illustration requiring such page formatting. Estimated number of photographs is __________. Estimated total cost for photographs $ ___________.

Total Estimated Cost $ _________________.

The AUTHOR is cautioned that this is an estimated cost only and actual costs cannot be determined until the final manuscript is completed and the total number of final pages, including the alphabetical index, table of contents etc is determined.

PAYMENT: The method of payment shall be as follows:

One-third (1/3) of the total estimated cost shown above at the time the AUTHOR delivers their original draft manuscript to GPS.

One-third (1/3) of the total estimated cost shown above at the time the AUTHOR returns the edited draft manuscript to GPS.

Balance due (Total estimated cost minus amounts already paid) within 5 days after the final camera-ready manuscript is completely ready for printing.

This contract shall be binding upon the parties hereto, their heirs, successors, assigns, and personal representatives. This Contract shall be construed and enforced in accordance with the laws of the State of North Carolina.

AS WITNESS, the hand and seal of the said AUTHOR and Owner, GENEALOGY PUBLISHING SERVICE.

This _____ day of _____________ 19____

ATTEST:

______________________________ (Author's Witness)

______________________________ (Author)

______________________________ (GPS Witness)

______________________________ (Owner, Genealogy Publishing Service)

Page 2 of 2

QUESTIONNAIRE

Genealogy Publishing Service, 448 Ruby Mine Road, Franklin, NC 28734

Your purchase of this book suggests that you plan to publish a family book. **GPS** is interested in your plans, objectives and schedule for accomplishing this worthwhile project. By having answers to the following questions, **GPS** can better respond to any questions you may have and provide you the additional advice and guidance you may need to successfully and economically complete your project on schedule.

Please answer the following questions, circling answers where appropriate

Have you started writing your draft manuscript? . . . . Yes . . . . . No

Is your draft manuscript complete? . . . . Yes . . . . . No

Draft manuscript will be: . . . . Handwritten . . . . Typewritten . . On computer disk

Estimated number of pages in manuscript: . . . . ____________

Estimated number of photographs: . . . . ____________

Estimated number of maps, drawings, etc: . . . . ____________

Will you personally prepare the camera-ready manuscript? . . . . Yes . . . . . No

If no, will **GPS** be considered for preparation of the camera-ready manuscript? . . . . Yes . . . . . No

Will you personally prepare the alphabetical index? . . . . Yes . . . . . No

How many current names and addresses do you have of potential buyers of your book? . . . . ____________

Will you distribute a pre-publication notice? . . . . Yes . . . . . No

Would you like **GPS** to design, print and mail a pre-publication notice to your mailing list? Yes . . . . . No

Would you like to see sample pages of your manuscript prepared in camera-ready format? Yes . . . . . No
If yes, please send us copies of several pages of your manuscript. If you are using a computer, please send us a disk with one of your chapter files, along with a printout.

Working title of your book: ____

Estimated number of books to be printed: . . . . ____________

Page trim size (see printing costs on page 28): . . . . . . 6" x 9" . . . . 7" x 10" . . . . 8½" x 11"

Hard cover or Soft cover (see printing costs on page 28): . . . . Hard . . . . Soft

Do you want the book copyrighted? . . . . Yes . . . . . No
(**GPS** will do this for you at no additional charge.)

Do you want a Library of Congress Card Catalog Number? .... Yes ..... No
(**GPS** will do this for you at no additional charge.)

Do you wish **GPS** to mail books directly to those who pre-ordered? .... Yes ..... No

If yes, will **GPS** store the remainder of the books, or ship them to you? .... Store .... Ship

Do you have a printing deadline for a reunion or other event, and what is that date? ____________

____

Will your book be financed solely by you or by a family association? ____________

If you are using a computer, please describe your equipment

Make and model of computer: ____________

Name and version of programs used to prepare manuscript: ____________

____

Type of printer you are using: ____________

Additional questions that GPS can answer for you

____

____

____

____

Name: ____________

Address: ____________

City/State/ Zip: ____________

Telephone: ____________

Date: ____________

Thank you for taking the time to fill out our questionnaire.

Our best wishes for a successful and timely completion of your project.